项目来源：新建院校改革与发展研究中心重点项目（项目编号：XJYX2020A02）
项目名称：产教融合背景下新建本科院校教师队伍转型发展研究——基于"双向多元"模式的探索
项目来源：四川省教育信息化应用与发展研究中心一般项目（项目编号：JYXX19-035）
项目名称：四川省属高校干部信息化领导力的提升机制研究——基于SEM的实证分析

四川新建本科院校行政人员工作绩效提升机制研究

彭 万 著

吉林大学出版社

·长春·

图书在版编目(CIP)数据

四川新建本科院校行政人员工作绩效提升机制研究 = Research on the Job Performance Improvement Mechanism of Administrative Staff in Newly-established Universities in Sichuan：英文 / 彭万著. -- 长春：吉林大学出版社，2020.7
ISBN 978-7-5692-6700-6

Ⅰ. ①四… Ⅱ. ①彭… Ⅲ. ①高等学校－行政管理－工作人员－人力资源管理－研究－四川－英文 Ⅳ. ① G647.23

中国版本图书馆 CIP 数据核字 (2020) 第 120829 号

书　　名：四川新建本科院校行政人员工作绩效提升机制研究
SICHUAN XINJIAN BENKE YUANXIAO XINGZHENG RENYUAN GONGZUO JIXIAO TISHENG JIZHI YANJIU

作　　者：彭　万　著
策划编辑：邵宇彤
责任编辑：代景丽
责任校对：杨　平
装帧设计：优盛文化
出版发行：吉林大学出版社
社　　址：长春市人民大街 4059 号
邮政编码：130021
发行电话：0431-89580028/29/21
网　　址：http://www.jlup.com.cn
电子邮箱：jdcbs@jlu.edu.cn
印　　刷：定州启航印刷有限公司
成品尺寸：170mm×240mm　16 开
印　　张：15.75
字　　数：305 千字
版　　次：2020 年 7 月第 1 版
印　　次：2020 年 7 月第 1 次
书　　号：ISBN 978-7-5692-6700-6
定　　价：62.00 元

版权所有　　翻印必究

Abstrak

Universiti yang baru ditubuhkan di Sichuan memainkan peranan penting dalam pembangunan zon ekonomi Chengdu-Chongqing yang mencatatkan pertumbuhan ekonomi keempat terbesar dan merupakan enjin pembangunan negara China. Walaubagaimanapun, prestasi kerja kakitangan pentadbiran dan anteseden berkaitannya setakat ini kurang mendapat perhatian dan keprihatinan dalam kedua-dua amalan pengurusan dan penyelidikan akademik. Kajian-kajian yang dijalankan sebelum ini mendapati terdapat perhubungan antara tanggapan sokongan organisasi dan penglibatan kerja dengan prestasi kerja. Kajian ini dijalankan untuk menyiasat pembolehubah yang mungkin dapat menjelaskan prestasi kerja kakitangan pentadbiran dengan menentukan hubungan antara tanggapan sokongan organisasi, penglibatan dan prestasi kerja. Kaedah kuantitatif digunakan untuk meneroka hubungan. Teknik pensampelan kluster digunakan dalam tinjauan dan data dikumpul melalui borang soal selidik yang diisi sendiri, dengan menggunakan skala tanggapan sokongan organisasi, skala penglibatan kerja Utrecht dan Skala prestasi kerja digunakan untuk mengukur pemboleh ubah dan dimensi yang berkaitan. Seramai 426 kakitangan akar umbi telah mengambil bahagian dalam soal selidik yang dijalankan. SPSS dan AMOS digunakan untuk menjalankan proses analisis data, dan hipotesis diuji dengan menggunakan pemodelan persamaan struktur. Keputusan menunjukkan tahap tanggapan sokongan organisasi (min=2.78, SD=0.69), penglibatan kerja (min=2.70, SD=0.72), dan prestasi kerja (min=2.53, SD=1.04) dalam kalangan kakitangan pentadbiran secara relatif adalah rendah. Sokongan organisasi dan penglibatan kerja memberi kesan positif terhadap pencapaian kerja. Keputusan kajian juga mendedahkan bahawa kesan tanggapan sokongan organisasi terhadap prestasi kerja dikawal oleh penglibatan kerja. Selain itu, hubungan pengantara antara dimensi tanggapan sokongan organisasi, dimensi penglibatan kerja dan dimensi prestasi kerja turut diperiksa. Kajian ini mencadangkan agar kakitangan pentadbiran universiti yang baru ditubuhkan diberi lebih sokongan material dan spiritual untuk mewujudkan budaya dan persekitaran yang melibatkan pekerja. Secara khususnya, pelbagai pendekatan yang melibatkan kebajikan pekerja perlu diambil untuk menunjukkan pihak universiti menghargai kakitangan pentadbiran. Kajian ini juga berfungsi sebagai latar belakang teori untuk penyelidikan lanjut.

Kata Kunci: Tanggapan sokongan organisasi, Penglibatan kerja, Prestasi kerja, Kakitangan pentadbiran, Universiti yang baru ditubuhkan

Abstract

Newly-established universities of Sichuan play an important role in the development of the Chengdu-Chongqing economic zone which is the fourth largest economic growth in China and regarded as a new engine of Chinese development. However, the job performance of administrative staff and its antecedents in newly-established universities have thus far received less attention and concern in both practice management and academic research. Previous studies found that perceived organizational support and work engagement have some relationship to job performance. This study is undertaken to investigate the job performance of administrative staff by determining the relationship between perceived organizational support, engagement and job performance. The quantitative method is employed. Cluster sampling technique is employed in the survey and data are collected via self-administered online questionnaires, utilizing perceived organizational support scale, Utrecht work engagement scale and job performance scale. A total of 426 administrative staffs participated in the survey. SPSS and AMOS are utilized to conduct the process of data analysis, and hypotheses are tested by using structural equation modeling. The results indicate that the level of perceived organizational support (mean=2.78, SD=0.69), work engagement (mean=2.70, SD=0.72), and job performance (mean=2.53, SD=1.04) among grassroots administrative staff is relatively low. Organizational support and work engagement have a significant positive effect on job performance. The findings also reveal that the effect of perceived organizational support on job performance is mediated by work engagement. Furthermore, the modeling relationship among dimensions of perceived organizational support, dimensions of work engagement and dimensions of job performance are examined. The study suggests giving more material and spiritual support to university administrative staff and create an engaged culture and atmosphere. In particular, diverse human care should be provided to show that universities identify the value of administrative staff. The study also serves as a theoretical background for further research.

Keywords: Perceived organizational support, Work engagement, Job performance, Administrative staff, Newly-established university

Table of Contents

CHAPTER ONE: INTRODUCTION ··· 001

    1.1 Introduction of the Study ··· 001

    1.2 Background of Study ··· 002

    1.3 Problem Statement ··· 005

    1.4 Objectives of the Study ··· 010

    1.5 Research Questions ··· 011

    1.6 Research Hypotheses and Conceptual Framework ··· 011

    1.7 Significance of the Study ··· 020

    1.8 Definitions of Newly-established University and Grassroots Administrative Staff · 022

    1.9 Limitations of the Study ··· 026

    1.10 Summary ··· 027

CHAPTER TWO: LITERATURE REVIEW ··· 028

    2.1 Introduction ··· 028

    2.2 Job Performance ··· 028

    2.3 Perceived Organizational Support ··· 033

    2.4 Work Engagement ··· 038

    2.5 Underlying Theories and Theoretical Framework ··· 048

    2.6 Past Empirical Studies ··· 059

    2.7 Summary ··· 073

CHAPTER THREE: RESEARCH METHODOLOGY · 074

    3.1   Introduction · 074

    3.2   Research Design · 076

    3.3   Sampling · 077

    3.4   Instrumentation · 086

    3.5   Data Collection · 097

    3.6   Study Ethics · 102

    3.7   Data Analysis Techniques · 102

    3.8   Pilot Study · 106

    3.9   Summary · 113

CHAPTER FOUR: DATA ANALYSIS AND RESULTS · 115

    4.1   Introduction · 115

    4.2   Response Rate · 115

    4.3   Data Preparation and Screening · 117

    4.4   Testing Non-response Bias · 123

    4.5   Descriptive Analysis · 125

    4.6   Multicollinearity/Correlation Matrix Test · 129

    4.7   Testing the Goodness of the Measurement Instrument · 131

    4.8   Hypothesized Structural Model · 152

    4.9   Hypotheses Test · 156

    4.10 Summary · 173

CHAPTER FIVE: DISCUSSION AND CONCLUSION · 174

    5.1   Introduction · 174

    5.2   Recapitulations of Research Findings · 174

    5.3   Discussions of Research Findings · 176

    5.4   Contributions of the Study · 181

5.5   Suggestions and Implications in Management ··· 185

5.6   Future Research ··· 187

5.7   Summary ··· 188

References ··· 190

APPENDIX 1: Survey Questionnaire ·· 233

SECTION A: Demographic Profile of the Respondents ····················· 234

SECTION B: Questionnaire ·· 235

CHAPTER ONE: INTRODUCTION

1.1 Introduction of the Study

The concept of job performance is very important both in management and academic field, and has been widely discussed for a long time. In simple terms, it refers to the evaluation of a person's work (Campbell, McCloy, Oppler and Sager, 1993). Academically, it is a part of human resources management and part of industrial and organizational psychology. Job performance is an essential criterion for evaluating organizational outcomes and job outcomes (Campbell, 1990). Job performance is the purpose and premise of the operation and development of any business and organization (Ding, 2002). Therefore, how to improve the job performance of employees has always been a major concern of academic research field in the world.

Under this background, research on the impact of organizational factors such as perceived organizational support, salary satisfaction, job satisfaction, leadership style and organizational commitment on job performance has become a hot topic for scholars (Luo, 2014). With the popularization of the concept and theory of perceived organizational support in the academia, perceived organizational support is considered as a critical factor in improving job performance of employees (Caesens and Stinglhamber, 2014; Rhoades and Eisenberger, 2002). There is some empirical research which indicated that perceived organizational support has a positive influence on job performance (Afzali, Motahari, Chen and Yin,

2009; Hatami-Shirkouhi, 2014; Mohamed and Ali, 2015), whereas some research revealed that perceived organizational support could not affect job performance significantly, unless it is mediated by other variables (Chiang and Hsieh, 2012). Moreover, some researchers found that perceived organizational support cannot influence job performance among particular populations (Labrague, McEnroe Petitte, Leocadio, Van Bogaert and Tsaras, 2018). It reveals that the effect of perceived organizational support on job performance may be different among different sample population in diverse organizational culture background.

On the other hand, work engagement which first appeared as a concept in management theory in the 1990s (Kahn, 1990), is also a fundamental construct for organizations to enhance their performance and get a competitive advantage (Cesário and Chambel, 2017; Xanthopoulou, Bakker, Demerouti and Schaufeli, 2009). However, very few people associate job performance with perceived organizational support and work engagement to study the relationship between the three constructs, and work engagement is rarely a concern of academia as mediation between perceived organizational support and job performance. Furthermore, education departments, educational leaders, and academics seldom think about how to effectively improve education management from the relationship between these three constructs. In this study, the constructs of perceived organizational support, work engagement, and job performance are put together to study their mutual relations on the context of Chinese newly-established universities, and this is a brand-new academic attempt.

1.2　Background of Study

In 2018, the *Chinese Higher Education Quality Report* proclaimed that many new universities and colleges had been created in China since 2000. According to the statistics, there were 1219 universities in China by the end of 2017, including 678 newly-established universities and undergraduate colleges. These newly-established universities and undergraduate colleges account for 55.6% of the total number of Chinese universities (Higher Education Evaluation Center of the Ministry of Education, 2018). Newly-built universities and undergraduate colleges have become an essential part of Chinese higher education institutions, and the improvement of their administration level is of considerable significance to the advancement of the level of Chinese higher education (Wang, 2016; Zhang and Xie, 2015). In Sichuan Province, for example, there are a total of 22 newly-established universities (not including 9 newly-established dependent colleges) to meet the needs of education, economic and social development.

On 30th May 2011, *The Development Plan of the Chengdu-Chongqing Economic Zone* (Chinese National Development and Reform Commission, 2011) was issued in China. According to the development plan, Chengdu-Chongqing Economic Zone contains the Sichuan Province and Chongqing Municipality; this zone is considered to be the fourth largest economic growth pole of China and the engine of Chinese western development (Wang, 2011).

Newly-established universities of Sichuan Province are closely related to the regional development of the economy, culture, education, science of Chengdu-Chongqing Economic Zone, and are very important in the development plan of Chengdu-Chongqing Economic Zone (Wang, 2011, 2016). These universities connect their professional construction with the development of local industries, take the road of integration of production, study and research, deepen the cooperation between universities and local governments, and transform to the application-oriented, thus deeply serving the development of the Chengdu-Chongqing Economic Zone. Cooperation between higher education and the economy continues to expand (Qiu, Zhang and Liu, 2016). For example, Yibin City in Sichuan Province is vigorously building a university town. The government has signed a project cooperation agreement with 11 universities. It can be said that with the rapid development of Chinese higher education and the local development needs of the Chengdu-Chongqing Economic Zone, the construction and development of newly-established universities are gradually becoming a hot topic in both academic and practical area (Qiu, Zhang and Liu, 2016; Wang, 2016).

The administration of universities is essentially a derivative activity of higher education (Yang, 2007). It follows the emergence of universities and develops along with the development of universities (Yang, 2007). On 5th September 2017, Sichuan Provincial Department of Education has released an important document named the *13th Five-Year Plan for educational development of Sichuan Province (From 2016 to 2020)* (Sichuan Provincial Department of Education, 2017). The document put forward in accordance with the standards which are "firmly faithful, service-oriented, diligent and pragmatic, responsible, clean and honest," to create a high-quality administrative team with proper management and service abilities. Therefore, it can be seen that the administrative team of newly-established universities in Sichuan has its own significance for improving the overall level of Sichuan higher education and even the development of education in Chengdu-Chongqing economic zone.

In the administrative team of universities, the proportion of grassroots administrative staff is the largest, and plays an important role. In 1985, *Trial Measures for the Establishment of Ordinary Institutions of Higher Education* (Chinese Education Ministry, 1985) defined the university administrative staff as people who engage in the administration at all levels of functional sections and departments of universities. Administrative staff can be divided into three levels: senior (decision-making level), middle (management level), grassroots (operational level) (Ding, 2009; Xu, 2007).

Ding (2009) stated in his paper *Research on the Incentive Mode of Grassroots Administrators in Universities* that grassroots administrative staff in universities is the main groups engaged in the administrative work of universities, and play an essential role in the operation of administration of universities, but it is clear that their job performance needs to be improved. Peng (2016) also argued that the administrative staff at the grassroots level, is an essential human resource team in colleges and universities; their engagement and performance can affect the administrative efficiency and development of higher education. However, compared with old or key universities, there are some problems in newly-established universities such as lack of running experience, lack of teacher resources, lack of office conditions and weak management system, which pose a more significant challenge to the administration, and oblige the administrative staff to assume more enormous tasks and pressures (Zhou, 2009). Taking into account the important role of grassroots administrative staff in the construction and development of newly-established universities as well as the important role played by Sichuan's newly-established universities in higher education system in Sichuan and Chengdu-

Chongqing economic zones, this study aims to explore the antecedent variables of job performance from the perspective of the interaction of organizational and individual factors, in order to find suitable ways to improve job performance of grassroots administrative staff. It can contribute to enhancing the newly-established universities' administration. Besides, the researcher is also a member of the grassroots administrative staff and engaged in human resource management in one of the newly-established universities in Sichuan. His job status and experience have given him a strong interest in this research and can provide him convenience during research and investigation. Furthermore, this research has practical guiding significance for the researcher's future work.

1.3 Problem Statement

There is an increasing contribution in academic and management area on the concepts of perceived organizational support, work engagement and job performance. However, in connection with this study, there are still some research problems.

The first problem is that the job performance of university administrative staff in China must be strengthened (Dong and Ma, 2013; Gao, 2015; Yu and Liu, 2013). This problem is receiving attention in the education management area recently, but the relevant research on it is not rich in academic circles. The *13th Five-Year Plan for Educational Development of Sichuan Province (From 2016 to 2020)* (Sichuan Provincial Department of Education, 2017) pointed out that the job performance of administrative staff is a big issue influencing the development of universities, and should be improved by human resource management practice and reform. Also, many scholars argue that the job performance of administrative staff is essential to the development of Chinese universities, and must be emphasized and strengthened (Dong and Ma, 2013; Gao, 2015; Si, 2010; Yu and Liu, 2013). However, the academic exploration of improving the job performance of university administrators is scarce (Yang, 2017). It is essential to explore the formation mechanism of job performance and find a path to enhance the job performance of university administrative staff.

Secondly, the current research on the relationship among three constructs (perceived organizational support, work engagement and job performance) is still limited, which needs to be further studied. More specifically, few researchers link job performance with perceived organizational support and work engagement together to investigate the relationship between the three constructs. Besides, the construct of work engagement is infrequently concerned by academia as mediation between perceived organizational support and job performance. In order to explore and find ways to improve employees' job performance, many studies connected to job performance with organizational commitment, organizational identity, employee satisfaction, human resources practice or other factors, but past studies seldom associate the work engagement with the relationship between perceived organizational support and job performance. As the earliest researcher of perceived organizational support, American researchers Eisenberger, Huntington, Hutchison and Sowa (1986) surveyed employees from 9 different industry organizations and found that perceived organizational support negatively correlated with absenteeism, and positively related to job performance. Since then, many global scholars began to do relevant studies. European scholars Caesens and Stinglhamber (2014) administrated an online questionnaire to 265 employees and 112 supervisors of companies, and found that perceived organizational support is positively related to work on engagement. Wang, Liu, Zou, Hao and Wu (2017) found that extrinsic effort could reduce work engagement among Chinese female nurses, while perceived organizational support could enhance work engagement. Iranian researchers Afzali, Motahari and Hatami-Shirkouhi (2014) randomly selected nearly 300 employees from different banks in Iran for a study and found that perceived organizational support has a positive impact on organizational learning and job performance. However, it is difficult to find studies of the relationship between three variables (perceived organizational support, engagement and job performance), and it is uncertain about whether a work engagement mediates the effect of organizational support on job performance. Therefore, as the above discussion, these still need to be further studied.

Thirdly, in-depth studies on the mutual influence of the dimensions of perceived organizational support, work engagement and job performance are still infrequent, especially studies on the mediating effect of work engagement mainly focused on a single mediator variable, few studies use multiple mediation model to perform complex mediation analysis of the dimensions of work engagement. Although some research has examined organization-related factors and personal factors as antecedents of job performance, they mostly take organizational factors, personal factors or job performance as a whole structural variable to conduct research (Buil, Martínez and Matute, 2019; Grobelna, 2019; Owens, Baker and Sumpter, 2016). Dividing variables into subdivisions and further exploring the relationships between the various dimensions through structural equations can help us understand the interaction between variables more deeply and thoroughly. Besides, the study on the mediating effect of work engagement mainly focused on a single mediator variable (Chaudhary Akhouri, 2018; Memon, Salleh, Nordin, Cheah, Ting and Chuah, 2018), namely simple mediation (Liu and Ling, 2009). However, nowadays, research is complex and often requires multiple mediators to more clearly explain the effects of independent variables on dependent variables (Mackinnon, 2008). Although more research on mediation has begun to conduct multiple mediation analysis in recent years, they just disassembled a multiple mediation model into several simple models, and then performed several simple mediation analyses (Fang, Wen, Zhang and Sun, 2014). Therefore, this study attempted to construct a multiple mediation structure model for multiple mediation analysis, which can analyze the relationship between multiple independent variables, multiple dependent variables and multiple mediator variables at the same time and same model, so as to gain a more in-depth insight into the mediating effects of the dimensions of work engagement.

Fourthly, there remains an academic knowledge gap in the literature, which continuously elicits the need for further empirical research of perceived organizational support, work engagement and job performance within diverse contexts and different demographic segments. It can be seen from past research that perceived organizational support, work engagement and job performance have been widely studied by the management field as well as the research/academic community and is regarded as the barometer that influences the association of the individual in the workplace. However, related empirical research infrequently involves the field of education management. As a particular demographic group, university administrative staff in China which has become a veritable higher education country, especially, did not receive much attention. Explicitly, this study attempts to fill this research gap. From the latest academic literature, Kim, Eisenberger, and Baik (2017) studied perceived organizational support and job performance with a sample of 109 small-to-medium sized South Korean firms, while DeConinck and DeConinck (2017) conducted a questionnaire survey of 382 salespeople in the United States to study whether servant leadership can predict the reception of organizational support and work results among salespeople. Akgunduz and Sanli (2017) collected data from hotels in Turkish cities to study the effect of employees' perceived organizational support for their performance. Labrague, McEnroe Petitte, Leocadio, Van Bogaert and Tsaras (2018) examined the impact of organizational support perceptions on nurses work outcomes. Guan and Frenkel (2017) used a survey on a sample of 455 employees working in five Chinese manufacturing firms to determine how work engagement mediates the relationship between employee perceptions of HR practice and job performance. From past research, the study of organizational support, work engagement, and job performance has involved business, medical, manufacturing, and tourism practitioners, but it has infrequently been involved in the education industry. In particular, researchers rarely pay attention to university administrators in their research (Kivistö and Pekkola, 2017). Further empirical research on the relationship between perceived organizational support, work engagement and job performance in diverse contexts and different demographic segments are needed.

Fifthly, as compared to the literature focusing on academic staff (or teachers), few studies have addressed problems of administrative staff, such as work status, work engagement, and job performance, whereas book chapters, papers or journal articles concerned about administrative staff in the context of higher education institutions are seldom existent, and this apparent lack of interest extends to policy and practice (Kivistö and Pekkola, 2017). For example, in *Standards and Guidelines for Quality Assurance in the European Higher Education Area*, which was revised in 2015, there is much more focus on the professional qualifications and competence development of teaching staff and effective information management practices. In China, *National Education Development Plan for 13th Five-Year* (Chinese State Council, 2017) has hardly mentioned the construction of the administrative team, and the development and quality assurance of administrative staff. Therefore, this study is prepared to address the existing knowledge gap, and arouse the attention and support of the academic, educational and management circles for administrative staff in higher institutions, and enhance understanding of and so further improve administrative staff's job performance.

The last problem is that the level of perceived organizational support, work engagement, and job performance of administrative staff in newly-established universities in the context of the rapid development of Chinese higher education is still unknown, and their relationship is uncertain. From the previous study, it is hard to find research which is devoted to investigating the above variables among administrative staff in newly-established universities of China. These issues require further investigation and research to get some valuable findings and implications. Yu, Liu and Liu (2013) pointed out that university leaders and higher education management authorities generally believe that teaching and academic work is the focus of the university; they attach importance to academic staff. In contrast, administrative staff, especially grassroots administrative staff is usually marginalized, and do not receive sufficient support from the university. Zhang's research (2016) on grassroots administrators in universities also argued that the universities' lack of support for grassroots administrators in terms of work environment, salary system, and professional growth reduce administrators' enthusiasm for work and thus reduce the efficiency of administrative work. Many people believe that the level of perceived organizational support, work engagement and job performance of university administrative staff is not high (Chen, 2017; Dong and Ma, 2013; Gao, 2015; Si, 2010; Yang, 2017; Yu, Liu and Liu, 2013). However, these conclusions are based only on people's observation, work experience, or interviews, lacking in quantitative information analysis as data support. Hence, it could benefit from using quantitative research to investigate perceived organizational support, work engagement and job performance of Chinese university administrative staff, and to broaden the perspective of education management by analyzing their mutual relations.

This study expands the research field of both human resources management and higher education management. It can enrich the method of research on the job performance of administrative staff in universities. In the context of the popularization of higher education in China and the Chengdu-Chongqing Economic Zone becoming China's fourth growth pole, the researcher chooses grassroots administrative staff in newly-established universities as a target population to explore the relationship between their perceived organizational support, work engagement and job performance, expecting to provide beneficial reference for university leaders and higher education management authorities so that they would consider how to improve the job performance of administrative staff from a new perspective.

1.4 Objectives of the Study

This study works to contribute to the understanding of whether or not the effect of different perceived organizational support on job performance may be reflective of the nature of work engagement in the Chinese context. Thus, the issue is whether or not work engagement mediates the impact of perceived organizational support on job performance. More specifically, the objectives of this study are:

1. To determine the level of job performance, perceived organizational support, and work engagement of grassroots administrative staff in newly-established universities in Sichuan, China.

2. To examine the relationship between perceived organizational support and job performance of grassroots administrative staff in newly-established universities in Sichuan, China.

3. To examine the relationship between perceived organizational support and work engagement of grassroots administrative staff in newly-established universities in Sichuan, China.

4. To examine the relationship between work engagement and job performance of grassroots administrative staff in newly-established universities in Sichuan, China.

5. To examine the mediating role of work engagement between perceived organizational support and job performance of grassroots administrative staff in newly-established universities in Sichuan, China.

1.5 Research Questions

In order to achieve the research objective, the following questions are proposed:

1. What is the level of job performance, perceived organizational support, and work engagement among grassroots administrative staff in newly-established universities in Sichuan, China?

2. Does perceived organizational support have a relationship with job performance among grassroots administrative staff in newly-established universities in Sichuan, China?

3. Does perceived organizational support have a relationship with work engagement among grassroots administrative staff in newly-established universities in Sichuan, China?

4. Does work engagement have a relationship with job performance among grassroots administrative staff in newly-established universities in Sichuan, China?

5. Does work engagement mediate the relationship between perceived organizational support and job performance of grassroots administrative staff in newly-established universities in Sichuan, China?

1.6 Research Hypotheses and Conceptual Framework

The purpose of this study is to examine the relationship between perceived organizational support, work engagement and job performance of grassroots administrative staff in newly-established universities in Sichuan, China. It furthers examine the mediation role of work engagement between perceived organizational support and job performance and then makes hypotheses and builds the conceptual framework. All hypotheses are listed below:

H1: Perceived organizational support is positively related to job performance of grassroots administrative staff in newly-established universities.

H1.1: Working support is positively related to task performance.

H1.2: Working support is positively related to contextual performance.

H1.3: Identifying value is positively related to task performance.

H1.4: Identifying value is positively related to contextual performance.

H1.5: Caring about well-being is positively related to task performance.

H1.6: Caring about well-being is positively related to contextual performance.

H2: Perceived organizational support is positively related to work engagement of grassroots administrative staff in newly-established universities.

H2.1: Working support is positively related to vigor.

H2.2: Working support is positively related to dedication.

H2.3: Working support is positively related to absorption.

H2.4: Identifying value is positively related to vigor.

H2.5: Identifying value is positively related to dedication.

H2.6: Identifying value is positively related to absorption.

H2.7: Caring about well-being is positively related to vigor.

H2.8: Caring about well-being is positively related to dedication.

H2.9: Caring about well-being is positively related to absorption.

H3: Work engagement is positively related to job performance of grassroots administrative staff in newly-established universities.

H3.1: Vigor is positively related to task performance.

H3.2: Vigor is positively related to contextual performance.

H3.3: Dedication is positively related to task performance.

H3.4: Dedication is positively related to contextual performance.

H3.5: Absorption is positively related to task performance.

H3.6: Absorption is positively related to contextual performance.

H4: Work engagement has a positive mediating effect in the relationship between perceived organizational support and job performance of grassroots administrative staff in newly-established universities.

H4.1: Vigor has a positive mediating effect in the relationship between working support and task performance.

H4.2: Vigor has a positive mediating effect in the relationship between working support and contextual performance.

H4.3: Vigor has a positive mediating effect in the relationship between

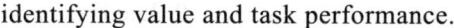

identifying value and task performance.

H4.4: Vigor has a positive mediating effect in the relationship between identifying value and contextual performance.

H4.5: Vigor has a positive mediating effect in the relationship between caring about well-being and task performance.

H4.6: Vigor has a positive mediating effect in the relationship between caring about well-being and contextual performance.

H4.7: Dedication has a positive mediating effect in the relationship between working support and task performance.

H4.8: Dedication has a positive mediating effect in the relationship between working support and contextual performance.

H4.9: Dedication has a positive mediating effect in the relationship between identifying value and task performance.

H4.10: Dedication has a positive mediating effect in the relationship between identifying value and contextual performance.

H4.11: Dedication has a positive mediating effect in the relationship between caring about well-being and task performance.

H4.12: Dedication has a positive mediating effect in the relationship between caring about well-being and contextual performance.

H4.13: Absorption has a positive mediating effect in the relationship between working support and task performance.

H4.14: Absorption has a positive mediating effect in the relationship between working support and contextual performance.

H4.15: Absorption has a positive mediating effect in the relationship between identifying value and task performance.

H4.16: Absorption has a positive mediating effect in the relationship between identifying value and contextual performance.

H4.17: Absorption has a positive mediating effect in the relationship between caring about well-being and task performance.

H4.18: Absorption has a positive mediating effect in the relationship between caring about well-being and contextual performance.

1. The hypothesis of relationship between perceived organizational support and job performance of grassroots administrative staff in newly-established universities

Perceived organizational support is based on the Existence, Relatedness and Growth theory or better known as ERG theory (Alderfer, 1972), and the relationship between perceived organizational support and job performance is deduced by the norm of reciprocity. Employees have three needs which are existence, relatedness and growth. When employees feel the caring about well-being, identifying value and working support from the organization, their three needs will be met, they will be motivated to work hard, be loyal, and work with more enthusiasm as exchanges to better complete the task and improve job performance. According to the norm of reciprocity, when a person or organization contributes to each other, they also expect the other party to return to their contribution. This norm is used for the relationship between employees and organizations. The implication of perceived organizational support theory is to highlight that the organization's concern and focus on employees are an important starting point for employees who are reluctant to leave the organization and to fulfill their commitment to the organization (Luo, 2014).

Empirical studies (Akgunduz and Sanli, 2017; Armeli, Eisenberger and Fasolo et al.,1998; Eisenberger, Armeli and Rexwinkel, 2001; Kraimer and Wayne, 2004; Mohamed and Ali, 2015; Pearce and Herbik, 2004; Truss and Soane, 2012; Zhou and Mu, 2005) on the relationship between perceived organizational support and job performance have been explored and can be divided into two categories. One is to directly explore the relationship between the two factors, and another is to carry out research through the introduction of mediating or moderating variables. The results of the study are consistent with those of the theory of social exchange, and prove that there is a positive correlation between the two.

The administrative staff in universities is a special group of teachers in universities. This study divides the perceived organizational support into three dimensions: working support, identifying value and caring about well-being, and divides the job performance into two dimensions: task performance and contextual performance. The following hypotheses are made:

H1: Perceived organizational support is positively related to job performance of grassroots administrative staff in newly-established universities.

H1.1: Working support is positively related to task performance.

H1.2: Working support is positively related to contextual performance.

H1.3: Identifying value is positively related to task performance.

H1.4: Identifying value is positively related to contextual performance.

H1.5: Caring about well-being is positively related to task performance.

H1.6: Caring about well-being is positively related to contextual performance.

2. The hypothesis of relationship between perceived organizational support and work engagement of grassroots administrative staff in newly-established universities

According to previous research (Eisenberger, 2001; May, 2004), perceived organizational support may have a positive effect on employee engagement. Eisenberger (2001) showed that when employees believe that the organization will be concerned about their personal situation, they will be more dedicated. May (2004) argued that a supportive relationship can effectively predict employee engagement. Thus, perceived organizational support can give employees a sense of responsibility, and they will be more dedicated to working, improve the level of work engagement. On the contrary, when employees often do not feel the support from the organization, they may produce negative emotions and behavior, thus reducing the level of work engagement.

In this study, the grassroots administrative staff of the newly-established universities is selected as the research participants, and perceived organizational support is divided into three dimensions: working support, identifying value and caring about well-being. The work engagement includes vigor, dedication and absorption. Hence, the following hypotheses are made:

H2: Perceived organizational support is positively related to work on engagement of grassroots administrative staff in newly-established universities.

H2.1: Working support is positively related to vigor.

H2.2: Working support is positively related to dedication.

H2.3: Working support is positively related to absorption.

H2.4: Identifying value is positively related to vigor.

H2.5: Identifying value is positively related to dedication.

H2.6: Identifying value is positively related to absorption.

H2.7: Caring about well-being is positively related to vigor.

H2.8: Caring about well-being is positively related to dedication.

H2.9: Caring about well-being is positively related to absorption.

3. The hypothesis of relationship between work engagement and job

performance of grassroots administrative staff in newly-established universities

Kahn (1990) pointed out that the engagement would affect employee performance when he first proposed the concept of employee engagement. In recent years, some empirical research results also revealed that there might be a positive correlation between engagement and job performance. Macey (2011) pointed out that the employee's engagement perception promoted the emergence of engagement behavior, and engagement behavior would influence job performance through the construction of employee engagement value chain. In recent years, some empirical research results also confirmed that there is a positive correlation between employee engagement and job performance. Among them, the research result of Rich, Lepine and Crawford (2010) showed that even though the control of work input, job satisfaction, internal motivation and other variables change, the work engagement is still able to affect the job performance positively. Menguc (2013) believed that customers' evaluation of job performance of employees is positively related to work on engagement in the service industry relied on job need-resource theory. Based on previous studies findings, this study also hypothesizes that work engagement is positively related to job performance, and this would be further elaborated in the next Chapter.

This study divides engagement into vigor, dedication, and absorption, and divides job performance into task performance and contextual performance. The following hypotheses are made:

H3: Work Engagement is positively related to job performance of grassroots administrative staff in newly-established universities.

H3.1: Vigor is positively related to task performance.

H3.2: Vigor is positively related to task contextual performance.

H3.3: Dedication is positively related to task performance.

H3.4: Dedication is positively related to contextual performance.

H3.5: Absorption is positively related to task performance.

H3.6: Absorption is positively related to contextual performance.

4. The hypothesis of the mediating role of work engagement on the relationship between perceived organizational support and job performance of grassroots administrative staff in newly-established universities

In order to maintain the stability of teachers' team, China's newly-established universities put forward the slogan of 'to retain faculty by rewards, to retain faculty by emotion.' As for grass-roots administrative staff in newly-established universities, the emotional experience and remuneration are equally important. Many scholars have noticed the critical role of individual factors, such as emotion. Cha (2007) argued that employee engagement is the positive input of the staff to work. With the job involvement, employees have a perfect physical, cognitive and emotional state. Employees with a high-level of engagement will put most of their time and energy into their work, and are willing to develop with their own organizations, have a sense of identity and a sense of belonging to the organization, so they will naturally achieve good job performance.

Scholars and research institutions in China and abroad have been undertaking work engagement as their research focus (May, 2004; Luo, 2014; Wang, 2015). May's studies (2004) showed that mental state variables could play a mediating role in the relationship between job characteristics and work input. Work richness, superior support, job role adaptability, co-encouragement among colleagues and available work resources have a positive effect on job input, which is achieved through psychological safety, psychological significance and psychological availability. Luo (2014) took the high-level talents of research universities as research participants and studied that work engagement may play a partial mediating role in the process of working support for influencing on teaching performance and scientific research performance. Wang (2015) pointed out that employees are active organisms, and if the organization's reward for them is regarded as an external stimulus, employees will form a sense of overall feeling and judgment (overall reward perception), and then make decisions according to the inherent needs and external environmental information, then take actions (engagement); this actions will lead to work results (performance). It can be seen that engagement directly determines the work process and work results of the staff, which plays a proximal role in job performance, while the overall reward perception plays a distal role in job performance (Wang, 2015). In other words, the effect of work engagement on job performance is greater than organizational reward. Therefore, it can be inferred that even if the organization reward for employees reaches a high level, if work engagement does not work, there might be no excellent job performance. According to this, if organizational support is regarded as reward and identification, work engagement may play a mediating role between perceived organizational support and job performance.

Hence, this study puts forward the following assumptions about the relationship between perceived organizational support and job performance:

H4: Work engagement has a positive mediating effect in the relationship between perceived organizational support and job performance of grassroots administrative staff in newly-established universities.

H4.1: Vigor has a positive mediating effect in the relationship between working support and task performance.

H4.2: Vigor has a positive mediating effect in the relationship between working support and contextual performance.

H4.3: Vigor has a positive mediating effect in the relationship between identifying value and task performance.

H4.4: Vigor has a positive mediating effect in the relationship between identifying value and contextual performance.

H4.5: Vigor has a positive mediating effect in the relationship between caring about well-being and task performance.

H4.6: Vigor has a positive mediating effect in the relationship between caring about well-being and contextual performance.

H4.7: Dedication has a positive mediating effect in the relationship between working support and task performance.

H4.8: Dedication has a positive mediating effect in the relationship between working support and contextual performance.

H4.9: Dedication has a positive mediating effect in the relationship between identifying value and task performance.

H4.10: Dedication has a positive mediating effect in the relationship between identifying value and contextual performance.

H4.11: Dedication has a positive mediating effect in the relationship between caring about well-being and task performance.

H4.12: Dedication has a positive mediating effect in the relationship between caring about well-being and contextual performance.

H4.13: Absorption has a positive mediating effect in the relationship between working support and task performance.

H4.14: Absorption has a positive mediating effect in the relationship between working support and contextual performance.

H4.15: Absorption has a positive mediating effect in the relationship between identifying value and task performance.

H4.16: Absorption has a positive mediating effect in the relationship between identifying value and contextual performance.

H4.17: Absorption has a positive mediating effect in the relationship between caring about well-being and task performance.

H4.18: Absorption has a positive mediating effect in the relationship between caring about well-being and contextual performance.

5. Conceptual framework

Based on the above hypotheses, the following conceptual framework is proposed in this study (Figure 1.1). In the framework, perceived organizational support is divided into three dimensions: working support, identifying value and caring about well-being. Work engagement is divided into vigor, dedication and absorption, and job performance is divided into task performance and contextual performance respectively. Each dimension is a separate structural variable in the framework. The basic logic of the framework is: working support, identifying value and caring about well-being make grassroots administrative staff of the newly-established universities generates the cognition and feelings for organizational support. These cognition and feelings can directly and positively affect their task performance and contextual performance. On the other hand, they also can improve administrative staff's engagement, including their vigor, dedication and absorption, so that makes them achieve a better job performance indirectly.

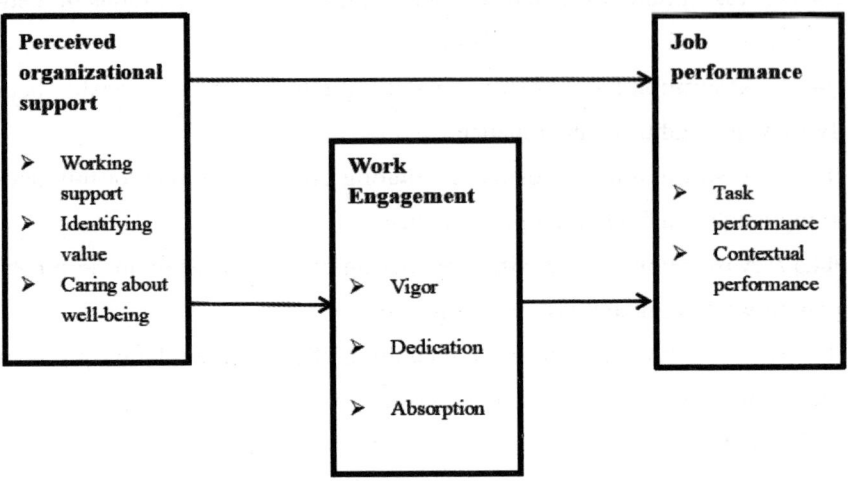

Figure 1.1. Conceptual Framework of the Study

1.7 Significance of the Study

1. This study enriches the literature on improving job performance and exploring the mediator of work engagement. Although many studies use perceived organizational support or work engagement as variables to study job performance, there is not much that explore work engagement as a mediation between perceived organizational support and job performance. In particular, this thesis not only studies the relationships between three variables of perceived organizational support, work engagement and job performance, but also studies the relationships between subdivisions, including working support, identifying value, caring about well-being, vigor, dedication, absorption, task performance and contextual performance. Furthermore, multiple mediation effects are also examined by the researcher. Analysis of multiple medications can provide a clearer explanation of the effects of independent variables on dependent variables (Mackinnon, 2008).

2. This study contributes to enriching the research field of both human

resources management and higher education management. In the context of the rapid growth of higher education in China, the number of newly-established universities is increasing. How to improve the administration level of newly-established universities by improving the performance of administrative staff is a valuable topic in the field of education management in China. In the research field of Chinese higher education management, the existing research on university administrative staff mostly adopts qualitative research methods, such as phenomenology, epistemology, case study, fieldwork, discourse analysis. Additionally, the study of the relationship between perceived organizational support, work engagement and job performance mostly focus on commercial and enterprise area, and most are under the background of Western cultural. In this study, grassroots administrative staff in newly-established universities, which is a special group, was selected as participants of the study, and quantitative research method was used to explore the relationship between their perceived organizational support, work engagement and job performance. It enriches the method of research on the job performance of administrative staff in Chinese universities, expands the context and target population of the study on the relationship between perceived organizational support, work engagement and job performance, and can make discoveries from new perspectives.

3. The research has significant value for improving the administration of universities. This paper summarizes the factors that affect the job performance of administrative staff by exploring the relationship between perceived organizational support, work engagement and performance, and helps the newly-established universities to adopt targeted strategies to improve the performance of grassroots administrative staff. By this way, the level of university administration can be improved.

4. The research helps to improve the practice of human resources management in newly-established universities. The administrative staff is a primary human resource of universities. The improvement of the job performance of grassroots administrative staff is an important task of human resource management in newly-established universities. Based on the thorough investigation and research, this study determines the level of performance of administrative staff in newly-established universities and explores the relationship between perceived

organizational support, work engagement and performance. This research can provide useful findings of data analysis and implication for the relevant government departments, leaders and policy-makers of the newly-established universities in China to formulate the strategic planning for administrative staff development and further deepen the human resource management system reform.

1.8 Definitions of Newly-established University and Grassroots Administrative Staff

1.8.1 Newly-established University

At present, the Chinese academic community defines the newly-established university based on these three different characteristics: the time of creation, owner-member relationship and development stage. According to the perspective of the time of creation, Gu (2012) defined newly-established university as higher education public or private institution which qualifies for undergraduate education. They were created by combination or independent upgrade since 2000, in which year Chinese higher education institutions' structure began to adjustment, universities began to expand the enrollment. From the perspective of the owner-member relationship, newly-established university is defined according to where the university is subordinate, as mentioned by Han (2009) mentioned in his paper: Newly-established universities refer to the comprehensive undergraduate universities which were established after 2000 and subordinate to province government, serve mainly for the local economic and social development. Another point of view of the definition of the newly-established university is from the perspective of university development stage. For example, Liu (2003) argued that the newly-established universities are higher education institutions which have a short history, still have no self-advantage in competition and development of Chinese universities. Zhang (2010) pointed out that the newly-established universities are a growing force under the background of general higher education development and reform in China.

In 2018, The *Chinese Higher Education Quality Report* proclaimed that a large number of universities and colleges have been born in China since 2000, which can be called newly-established universities and colleges, and account for 55.6% of the total number of Chinese universities (Higher Education Evaluation Center of the Ministry of Education, 2018). Therefore, newly-established universities in Sichuan, refer to public and private universities subordinated to Sichuan provincial government and founded since 1999 by way of upgrading or combination. This definition of newly-established universities is also consistent with the definition used by most of the researchers (Gu, 2012; Han, 2012; Liu, 2003; Zhang, 2010). Most of the newly-established universities are located in the prefecture-level cities. They are even the only universities in those cities. They have three prominent features. First is new, it means that they have a short build-development history. Second is that they are subordinate to the Sichuan provincial government. Third is that they are comprehensive undergraduate institutions.

It is important to point out that Chinese universities can be divided into three types by the establishment system: public universities, private universities, and independent colleges (Zhu and Lou, 2011). The public universities were established by a national government or local government. Private universities refer to universities or higher education institutions established by social organizations or individuals using non-state funds. Independent colleges are higher education institutions organized jointly by public universities and individual institutions (Zhu and Lou, 2011). The name of an independent college generally covers the name of the parent university, such as the "××University ×× College", which is the main feature that distinguishes the independent college from other universities (Zhang, 2011).

In this study, the newly-established universities in Sichuan, refer to public and private universities subordinated to Sichuan provincial government and founded since 1999 by way of upgrading or combination. Newly-established independent colleges are not included in this study because their systems are quite different from other universities.

1.8.2 Grassroots Administrative Staff

The definition of grassroots administrative staff in universities is related to administrative post and grade system in Chinese higher institution. Chinese Education Ministry Document Guidance on the Implementation of Post Setting and Management in Colleges and Universities (Chinese Education Ministry, 2007) divides the faculty into three categories: Administrative, Academics and Logistics.

In 1985, Trial Measures for the Establishment of Ordinary Institutions of Higher Education (Chinese Education Ministry, 1985) defined the university administrative staff as people who engage in the administration at all levels of functional sections and departments of universities. In 2008, The Implementation Opinions on the Post Setting Management of Institutions in Sichuan Province (Sichuan Provincial Government, 2008) clearly stipulate that administrative posts in university refer to jobs engaged in administrative tasks. Academic posts refer to jobs engaged in professional and technical work such as teaching and scientific research. The administrative and academic posts are not allowed to overlap each other. A staff member can only occupy one position in the university.

According to Opinions on the Implementation of Post Setting and Management in Institutional Organization (Chinese National Human Resources Ministry, 2006) issued by Chinese National Human Resources Ministry, the administrative post in the institutional organization including university can be divided into 10 grades as shown by Table 1.1 below:

Table 1.1 *Administrative Post and Grade System of Institutional Organization in China (Chinese Education Ministry, 2007)*

Role	Administrative post	Grade
Leading roles of ministries or equivalents, or of provinces or equivalents	Bu	1
	Deputy Bu	2

Continued

Role	Administrative post	Grade
Leading roles of departments or equivalents, or of prefectures or equivalents, or consultants at the same level	Ting	3
	Deputy Ting	4
Leading roles of divisions or equivalents, or of counties or equivalents, or consultants at the same level	Chu	5
	Deputy Chu	6
Leading roles of sections or equivalents, or of townships or equivalents	Ke	7
	Deputy Ke	8
Staff members	None	9
Clerks	None	10

For the newly-established university, it is generally considered that administrative staff can be divided into three levels: senior (decision-making level), middle (management level), grassroots (operational level) (Ding, 2009; Xu, 2007). Corresponding to the table above, Senior administrative staff refers to Ting and Deputy Ting at 3-4 grades, the leading of university; and middle-level administrative staff refers to the Chu and Deputy Chu at 5-6 grades, the leaders of college or department of the university. Grassroots administrative staff refers to Ke and Deputy Ke and the following staff at 7-10 grades (Ding, 2009; Xu, 2007; Zhang, 2016). They are engaged in specific administrative work under the leadership, including academic affairs, research management, human resources management, financial management, infrastructure, library management, logistics services, and other management and service affairs in different departments.

Overall, grassroots administrative staff in this study refers to Ke, Deputy Ke and the following staff in newly-established universities. In other words, they are administrative staff at 7-10 administrative grades in newly-established universities. They are the main force of administrative work.

1.9　Limitations of the Study

1. This research used quantitative methodology with a questionnaire, which can only reveal the relationship between perceived organizational support, work engagement and performance of grassroots administrative staff in universities. However, it cannot accurately explain the problem of 'why' or 'how' behind the phenomenon and relationship.

2. The questionnaires used in this research are self-administered. Although this data collection method is widely used in the study of social sciences, subjective sensory is affected by personal and environmental influences, such as individual professions, values, university culture, which may lead to unreal responses. In addition, some participants may have scruples and reservations about their responses to the questions because of social expectations or psychological defenses. The questions of whether the participants can respond to the questionnaires honestly, and whether the participants can accurately evaluate themselves remain. These problems may affect the authenticity and reliability of the data collected. Future research may try to adopt a more objective and accurate method of investigation.

3. The research participants are limited to the grassroots administrative staff of the newly-established universities in Sichuan. There are a large number of Chinese universities, including 985, 211 project universities, old traditional universities, newly-established universities, the level and situation of each university are not the same. Even the newly-established universities in different provinces, due to the difference of location, running conditions, the quality of students, the level of scientific research and other aspects, their administrative level and human resources management model may be a bit different. Thus, the data analysis and results of this research are not necessarily applicable to other categories of universities. Besides, the grassroots administrative staff is an extraordinary group of university faculty, their personality and job characteristics are quite different from other faulty, so the data analysis and conclusions drawn from this study do

not necessarily apply to other types of faculty in colleges and universities, such as academic staff.

1.10 Summary

   This chapter introduces the unique background of this study, states the critical problems related to the study, raises five main questions and objectives. According to the questions and goals, four main hypotheses are put forward, including the hypotheses of the relationship between every two variables and hypothesis of the mediating variable. Based on the hypotheses, the conceptual framework is provided in this chapter, whereafter, the significance of the study, definitions of terms which are newly-established university and grassroots administrative staff, and limitation of the study is elaborated. After the introduction of this study by Chapter 1, Chapter 2 reviews and discusses relevant literature for this study.

CHAPTER TWO: LITERATURE REVIEW

2.1 Introduction

The purpose of this chapter is to review literature related to the research topic and research questions posed in Chapter 1. This chapter firstly reviews and concludes the operational definitions including job performance, perceived organizational support and work engagement. Secondly, this chapter discusses relevant underlying theories and constructs a theoretical framework to explain and support relevant variables and hypotheses of the relationship between variables. Thirdly, previous empirical studies are reviewed and discussed.

2.2 Job Performance

2.2.1 Background and Definition of Job Performance

Job performance, studied as part of human resources management academically, also forms a part of industrial and organizational psychology. The concept of job performance is critical both in practice management and academic field, and has been a major concern for a long time. In simple terms, it refers to the evaluation of a person's work (Campbell et al., 1993). Job performance is the purpose and premise of the operation and development of any enterprise, organization, including organizational performance and employee individual performance (Ding, 2002). Campbell (1990) describes job performance as a variable at the individual level, or as a single person performance. This distinguishes it from a more inclusive structure, such as organizational performance or national performance, which are higher-level variables. This research studies the relationship between perceived organizational support, work engagement and job performance of grassroots administrative staff in newly-established universities. Thus, the research focuses on the employee performance at the individual level. Table 2.1 presents several representative definitions of employee performance at the individual level.

Table 2.1 *The Definitions of Job Performance Given by Researchers*

Year	Researcher	Definition
1968	Porter and Lawler	Job performance is made up of the quantity of performance, the quality of performance, and the degree of work effort.
1986	Hall and Goodale	Employee performance is a way for employees to work on their own, including their own arrangement of learning, technical skills, interaction with others, obedience to leadership, etc.
1993	Campbell	Job performance is different from effect or productivity. Employee performance involves the performance of the individual, etc. The effect involves assessing performance results, and productivity means how the individual or organization behaves.

Continued

Year	Researcher	Definition
1994	Byars and Rue	Job performance refers to the net effect of employee effort, influenced by the ability of employees and the role cognition. This means that in a particular case, employee performance can be seen as the result of the relationship between effort, competency, and role cognition.
1997	Borman and Motowidlo	Employee performance is assessable, multi-dimensional, continuous behavioral structure associated with organizational goals.
2002	Rotundo and Sackett	Job performance is a result of individual achievement at a particular time in some way

From the table above, it can be seen that different researchers have different definitions of job performance. Job performance is one of the most popular issues in the field of organizational behavior and human resource management. It does not have a unified definition, just as many other concepts in human resource management. At first, the study of scholar's interpretation of job performance mainly includes two views: one view is to regard the performance as a result; the other view is to consider performance as individual behavior. However, the subsequent study of the 1990s began to define job performance as multidimensional, believing that job performance is not only a result but also related behavior to achieve these results, including brainwork and physical labor required to achieve the results of the work. Therefore, different scholars put forward different definitions of job performance from different angles according to their research.

1. Bermardin et al. (1984) defined job performance as a record of specific job activities at a particular period; This definition typically equates performance with results.

2. Campbell (1990) argued that job performance is an employee's behavior at work and this behavior must contribute to the achievement of an organization's goals. He believes that job performance is what people do for the realization of the organization's goal and can be observed. He believes that job performance is synonymous with behavior and should be separated from the results (Luo, 2014). Schneider (1995) argued that job performance is what an individual or system does and that behavior is important in the process of accomplishing the task.

3. Performance is not just a complete result, not just behavior to achieve the goal, but the combination of the two (Chen and Duan, 2008). Brumbrach (1988) argued that performance is behavior and result. It is the behavior that employees put into their tasks. However, this behavior is not only the tool to achieve the results, but its own is also the result. It is the result of mental and physical effort to complete the task. Borman and Motowildo (1993) divided job performance into task performance and contextual performance, indicating that job performance is a unity of results and behavior.

In fact, different types of employees apply to different performance definitions and performance evaluations. Performance-oriented or output-oriented performance definition is more suitable for measuring sales staff, technician and other types of employees whose job performance can be quantified. Behavior-oriented performance definition is more appropriate to measure management and service staff and other types of employees whose job performance is difficult to be quantified but needs to emphasize the work process. It can be seen that the use of results or behavior individually to define job performance is not comprehensive. Combined with the previous study, job performance can be regarded as the behavior and results of the work of university administrative staff who is engaged in the administrative work of the university in order to realize the construction and development of universities. In general, it could be said that job performance evaluates whether or not a person is performing his job well.

2.2.2 Dimension of Job Performance

From the previous study, most researchers divided job performance into two dimensions: task performance and contextual performance (Borman and

Motowidle, 1993; Özçelİk and Uyargil, 2019; Scotter and Motowidlo, 1994; Wang, Li and Luo, 2007).

Borman and Motowidle (1993) has made outstanding contributions to the research on job performance. In their study, Borman and Motowidle (1993) firstly divided job performance into two dimensions: task performance and contextual performance, which are the basis for future research on job performance. The focus of task performance is the degree of skill proficiency required to complete the task, and the degree of achievement of the goal. Contextual performance emphasizes the interpersonal relationships of organizational members, organizational atmosphere, and organizational environment, organization's social network and the psychological climate which can support task performance.

In order to further study the two-dimensional structure model of job performance, Scotter and Motowidlo (1994) took the air force mechanics as the research participants, and studied the difference between the organization's task and contextual performance dimension of the air force mechanics group through the superior evaluation method. The results show that there are significant differences in task performance and contextual performance of the air force mechanics group, which affects the overall performance individually, and the correlation between the contextual performance and the individual characteristics of the sample studies is higher.

Wang, Li, and Luo (2007) used confirmatory factor analysis to the structural differences in task performance and contextual performance in the Chinese cultural context. The results show that task performance and contextual performance can be distinguished in the structure. It can be seen that the dual structure model of job performance in the Chinese cultural context is also applicable.

Based on the two-dimensional structure model of job performance, many scholars have further explored and expanded the dimension.

Scotter and Motowidlo (1996) divided contextual performance into interpersonal promotion and work dedication based on the distinction between task performance and contextual performance. The Chinese scholar Wen Zhiyi who takes managers at the middle level as the research object, explores the exploratory factor analysis (EFA) of their job performance, and divides the job performance into four dimensions: task performance, interpersonal performance, adaptability and effort performance (Chen and Duan, 2008). On the basis of summarizing the previous research, Han (2006) constructs a conceptual model of four-dimensional job performance through EFA. Based on task performance and contextual performance, Han (2006) also derives both learning performance and innovation performance. There are some progressive ascending relationships in these four dimensions (Hu, 2009).

The division of job performance has undergone a different process, which only focused on results in the beginning, that is, task performance, and later not only focused on results, but also paid attention to processes, that is, contextual performance, as well as learning performance which is controversial to a certain extent.

As the connotation and extension of job performance at different times and different organizational backgrounds are not the same, it is bound to involve the evolution of the dimensionality of job performance (Zhao, 2012). The job performance involved in this paper should be a comprehensive consideration of the characteristics of the administrative performance of universities, mainly to assess the performance of the results and the performance of the process. Moreover, the two dimensions of job performance, namely task and contextual performance, have received the most attention and acceptance from various scholars (Özçelik and Uyargil, 2019). Therefore, from the above discussion, it could be said that the job performance of administrative staff in universities is divided into two dimensions: task performance and contextual performance.

2.3 Perceived Organizational Support

2.3.1 The Background and Definition of Perceived Organizational Support

Global higher education has undergone tremendous changes over the past few decades. These kinds of changes occurred in the context of the accelerated development of science and technology and globalization, and have profoundly influenced the educational management model in various countries and regions (Maringe and Mourad, 2012). The previous stable relationship of university-teacher cooperation in the development of higher education is now facing a huge impact (Luo, 2014). Teacher resources, especially human resources have become the first resource of the organization, and many universities need to re-face the innovation of an employee-organization relationship, and strive to gain the development advantage in the existing international education market competition.

Employee-organization relationship reflects the characteristics of exchange. Barnard (2003) argues that an organization is a system that consciously coordinates the activities or theories of two or more people. The organization consists of people, and everyone in the organization has his or her own need. If the members are asked to contribute to the organization, the organization must provide them with incentives to meet their individual needs. Incentives include not only monetary and other material factors, but also prestige, power, participation in management and other social factors. Incentives and contributions must maintain a certain degree of balance in order to make the members of the organization have the appropriate willingness to cooperate. In this way, organizational goals can be achieved. If the incentive does not make the members feel balanced, the contribution of the members will be reduced or even withdrawn from the organization (Richardson, 2014).

Research on perceived organizational support began with the observation that if managers were concerned with their employees' commitment to the organization, employees focused on the organization's commitment to them (Eisenberger et al., 1986). In 1986, American psychologist Eisenberger pointed out that the academic community paid more attention to the commitment of the employees to the organization in discussing the relationship between the organization and the employees, but ignored the organization's commitment to employees. Thus, it resulted in a mismatched bidirectional relationship (Hayton, Carnabuci and Eisenberger, 2011).

Subsequently, Eisenberger (1986) and other researchers put forward the definition of perceived organizational support on the basis of organizational anthropomorphic thought and the norm of reciprocity. Perceived organizational support is the degree to which employees believe that their organization values their contributions and cares about their well-being and fulfills socioemotional needs (Eisenberger et al., 1986). The theory has two main points: one is the feelings of employees about whether the organization attaches importance to their contribution; the second is the feelings of employees about whether the organization is concerned about their happiness, including happiness of work and happiness of life (Xu, Che, Lin and Zhang 2005), Employee's perceived organizational support may also be assessed as a guarantee and assurance that employee can get help from the organization when he needs to work effectively and respond to stress situations (George, 1993).

Perceived organizational support has a tendency to make organization anthropomorphic. According to this view, Eisenberger et al.'s research (1986) shows that employees in the organization believe that the organization will pay attention to their contribution in work, and take this contribution as a reference to whether the organization should be concerned about the happiness of employees (Zhang, 2011). Perceived organizational support will, to some extent, guide the organization's impact on employees, as well as to measure the organization's assessment of the employees, resulting in a different attribution process. Different organizations will use different ways to treat employees, where employees will produce corresponding ideas in this process, and produce a sense of exchange (Jian, Wang and Tong, 2017). Employees will have such a belief in their minds. This belief is to rely entirely on organizational support to become own motive force and to measure organizational attitudes in specific perceptions (Shore and Tetrick, 1991; Shore and Wayne, 1993).

If the needs of employees can be effectively met, employees will have a positive view of the organization and play a greater potential in their work (Rhoades, Eisenberger and Armeil, 2002). A link to this study can be established as it can be said that the grassroots administrative staff in newly-established universities can perceive how their own universities support themselves, and this kind of perception can affect their work engagement and job performance in administrative work.

Perceived organizational support theory makes up for the shortcomings of previous research and practice, focusing only on employees' commitment to the organization, but ignoring the organization's commitment to the employees (Zhang,

2011). Ling, Yang and Fang (2006) argued that in the context of Chinese human resource management, organizational support is the sense that employees perceive their organization's support for their work, their interest and the recognition of their values. This shows that the positive impetus of perceived organizational support can be felt deeply by the employees.

Overall, perceived organizational support is the feeling of employees about their organizational support for themselves. In other words, it is the degree to which employees think that their working organization support for them (Eisenberger et al., 1986). Combining Eisenberge's (1986) definition of perceived organizational support from this study, perceived organizational support is the degree to which grassroots administrative staff believes that their own university values their contributions and cares about their well-being and fulfills their socio-emotional needs.

2.3.2 Dimensions of Perceived Organizational Support

In terms of the dimensions of perceived organizational support, the initial study found that it was a single dimension. This single dimension focuses primarily on emotional support such as intimate support and respect for support. Now when the academic community studies perceived organizational support, the trend is changed from one-dimensional form to multi-dimensional form, as showed in Table 2.2:

Table 2.2 *Division of Dimensions of Perceived Organizational Support Proposed by Researchers*

Researchers and years	Dimension	Details
Eisenberger (1986)	Single dimension	Emotional support
McMillin (1997)	Two-dimension	Instrumental support, and emotional support
Allen (2001)	Three-dimension	Instrumental support, emotional support, and superior support

Continued

Researchers and years	Dimension	Details
Kraimer, Wayne (2004)	Three-dimension	Adjustment organizational support, career organizational support, and financial organizational support
Ling Wenquan et al. (2006)	Three-dimension	Working support, identifying value, and caring about the well-being

From the above table, it can be seen that there are two different main views on the division of perceived organizational support dimensions.

Eisenberger et al. (1986) found out that perceived organizational support is one dimension variable through a large scale of the survey. This view is accepted by several researchers and this survey scale is widely used for related research in Western countries. On the contrary, more and more scholars proposed and believed that perceived organizational support is multidimensional. However, their opinions on the division of the dimensions are not consistent because of different research backgrounds and research methods (Wang, 2014). For instance, Allen (2001) divided perceived organizational support into instrumental support, emotional support and supervisor support, whereas Kraimer and Wayne (2004) proposed adjustment organizational support, career organizational support, and financial organizational support. In the context of Chinese organizational culture, vice president of Chinese Psychological Society, Ling, put forward three dimensions from the perspective of the role of organizational support, which is, working support, identifying value, and caring about well-being (Ling et al., 2006). His questionnaire is considered the Chinese culture as the background, and held that perceived organizational support of employees is a three-dimensional psychological structure. This kind of dimension division is more acceptable by researchers in the context of Chinese organizational culture. Zhang (2013) and Ma (2016) adopted Ling et al.'s dimensional division, namely working support, identifying value, and caring about well-being in the analysis and measurement of the perceived organizational support of employees in Chinese enterprises, Luo (2014), Liu and Li (2015) also adopted Ling et al.'s dimensional division in the research and measurement of perceived organizational support of Chinese higher institution teachers respectively. Therefore, this study also regards perceived organizational support as the three dimensions of working support, identifying value, and caring about well-being.

The organizational support of this three-dimensional structure reflects employees' work motivation, that is, the material security provided by the organization, recognition and respect in the organization, self-achievement in work, which is closer to the psychological status quo of administrative staff in newly-established universities. Therefore, this study uses working support, identifying value, and caring about well-being to measure perceived organizational support, which will be further elaborated and validated in Chapter 3.

2.4 Work Engagement

2.4.1 Background and Definition of Work Engagement

Kahn (1990) first proposed the concept of engagement. It can be seen from the literature review that there are usually two ways to understand the engagement in organizational behavior research. Scholars led by Kahn (1990) regard engagement as employee/individual engagement, while scholars represented by Schaufeli (2002) regard engagement as job/work engagement. This study focuses on engagement at work, a desirable condition for employees as well as for the organization they work for. Although typically 'employee engagement' and 'work engagement' are used interchangeably, this study prefers the latter, that is, work engagement because it is more specific. Work engagement refers to the relationship of the employees with their work, while employee engagement may also include the relationship with the organization (Schaufeli, 2013). Engagement in this study focuses on the relationship of the administrative staff with their work, hence the concept of 'work engagement' is used. However, literature on both work engagement and employee

CHAPTER TWO: LITERATURE REVIEW

engagement has been reviewed in this study in order to explore and understand the engagement in depth.

Researcher Kahn (1990) and company Gallup (2005) are the representatives of employee/personal engagement, while Schaufeli (2002) is the representative of work/job engagement, which usually appears in research related to job burnout and work stress. The concept of engagement was first proposed by Kahn (1990). Subsequently, scholars and researchers have given the definition of engagement from their respective research perspectives, and given the corresponding structural dimensions. Under Chinese cultural background, local and foreign scholars have come up with a lot of understanding and definitions of engagement, but so far there has not been a broad consensus. Even the words used to translate the engagement into Chinese are different. One translation is '敬业度' which is pronounced 'Jing Ye Du' (Luo, 2014; Yang, 2008) while another translation is '工作投入' pronounced 'Gong Zuo Tou Ru' (Cao, Peng and Liang, 2013; Hu and Wang, 2014).

Table 2.3 *The Definitions of Engagement Given by Researchers*

Researcher	Definition
Kahn (1990)	Personal engagement is the harnessing of organization members' selves to their work roles. In engagement, people employ and express themselves physically, cognitively, and emotionally during role performances.
Maslach and Leiter (1997)	Engagement and Job burnout are two extremes of the three-dimensional continuum. Engagement refers to a state of feeling that is full of energy and can effectively enter the working state and live in harmony with others.
Britt, Adler and Bartone (2001)	The employee's strong sense of mission and commitment to his work, and associates his sense of responsibility with job performance
Rothbard (2001)	Employee engagement represents the degree of employee's psychological input to the organization

Continued

Researcher	Definition
Schaufeli et al. (2002)	Work engagement is a psychological state assumed to be negatively related to burnout. It is defined as a positive, fulfilling, work-related state of minding.
Robinson (2004)	Work engagement is made up of commitment, organizational citizenship and motivation
May et al. (2004)	Job engagement can be considered a significant degree of the job state for a person, and it emphasizes how the employees of the organization invest themselves in the performance of the work, which includes not only the cognition, but also the flexible application of emotion and behavior.
Zeng and Han (2005)	Employee engagement is a lasting, positive mood and motive awakening to working, ready to be devoted to working, and accompanied by pleasure, pride and inspirational experience in the course of action. Not easy to feel tired during work. In the face of difficulties and pressure, have a high tolerance, once go into the role of work, do not want to get out of work, and are willing to make an effort for extra practice.
Xie (2006)	Work engagement is a sort of professional responsibility. It is not for an organization or a person, but is a professional spirit to assume a certain responsibility or engaged in a career.
Saks (2006)	Engagement is the degree to which individuals focus on their work and are immersed in the job role.

Continued

Researcher	Definition
Rich (2006)	Job engagement is a state of employee behavior, cognition, and affection.
Cha (2007)	Work engagement refers to the positive input of the employee at work, along with the complete physiological, cognitive and emotional state of the work
Macey and Schneider (2008)	Employee engagement is used at different times to refer to psychological states, traits, and behaviors as well as their antecedents and outcomes.
Shuck and Wollard (2009)	It refers to employees' cognitive, emotional and behavioral state for the desired results to the organization.
Yang (2012)	Work engagement is the mental state in which employees recognize their work and devote their time and energy to work and are willing to work with the organization.

The table above summarizing the definitions of engagement from the different perspective of scholars. In addition to scholars, there are many relevant organizations, consulting companies, and professional services firms which are also actively involved in the study of engagement, and gave the definitions of engagement from their own perspective. Table 2.4 summarizes the definitions of engagement proposed by representative companies and firms.

Table 2.4 *The Definitions of Engagement Given by Companies or Firms*

Company or firm	Definition
Gallup (2005)	Employee engagement is the degree of employee's emotional identity and work input to the organization.
Hewitt (2004)	Employee engagement is a measure of the willingness of employees to stay in the company and the effort to provide services for the company.
Towers Perrin (2003)	Employee engagement is the degree of willingness of employees to help organizations succeed in their business and the extent to which employees take practical action.
Hay Group (2009)	Refers to the result of stimulating the work enthusiasm of employees.
DDI (Development Dimensions International, 2005)	Work engagement means that employees are able to work in an environment that provides positive support for them. Meanwhile employees achieve their own value in the course of their work.

As can be seen from the above table, different researchers and companies have different understandings and interpretations of work engagement. Although the concept and dimensions of engagement have not achieved a unified understanding by scholars and organizations, the following consensus can be obtained by their studies and research:

Firstly, engagement is the result of the interaction of individual employees and their working roles. That means, if the individual employees do not work with their role, work/employee engagement is out of the question. For example, the definition of Kahn (1990) is based on the assumption that organizational members put themselves in the role of work. Schaufeli (2002) pointed out that engagement is "a positive, full of emotion and self-perceived state, and this mood and state are work-related" (p. 74).

Secondly, engagement is multidimensional. From definitions given by different researchers and firms, it can be seen that the multi-dimension of engagement has been universally accepted.

Thirdly, the realization of engagement is through the joint efforts of organizations and employees. In another word, work/employee engagement not only requires employees to understand organization's goals, to improve their performance with their colleagues for the interests of the company, but also requires the organization to promote, nurture and maintain employee engagement through its own operations.

In conclusion, engagement is actually the employee's emotional and intellectual input to the organization, and the employee's commitment to the organization. It is a reflection of the employee's sense of identifying, belonging and responsibility toward the organization (Tang, 2009). Based on a study by Kahn (1990), the concept of work engagement in this study refers to the job involvement of grassroots administrative staff in newly-established universities. It is the harnessing of university administrative staff's selves to their work roles: in engagement, administrative staff employs and expresses themselves physically, cognitively, emotionally during role performances.

2.4.2 Dimensions of Work Engagement

Because of different definitions of engagement in each study, the dimensions of engagement are also different. Table 2.5 summarizes the structural dimensions of engagement proposed by representative researchers.

Table 2.5 *Dimensions of Engagement Proposed by Researchers*

Researcher	Structural dimension
Kahn (1990)	1.Physical: employees can maintain the physical and energy in the implementation of the task; 2.Cognitive: employees not only understand their work mission and professional role, but also always keep the mind flexible, keep thinking clearly in work.

Continued

Researcher	Structural dimension
Kahn (1990)	3.Emotional: employees can actively communicate with others at work, and good at feeling the emotions of others.
Maslach and Leiter (1997)	1.Energy 2. Involvement 3.Efficacy
Britt, Adler and Bartone, (2001)	1.Perceived Responsibility 2. Commitment 3. Perceived influence of job performance
Rothbard (2001)	1. Concern: the effectiveness of employee awareness and the time and effort spent by employees in the role. 2. All inputs: the employees put all the energy into the role of work.
Schaufeli et al. (2002)	1.Vigor: That is willing to invest in energy for the work, and always maintain a full mental state at work, even if there are difficulties. 2.Dedication: employees are proud and satisfied with their work and have the courage to face the challenge; 3.Absorption: employees are completely immersed in the work, and it's hard to separate from work for them.
Zeng et al. (2005)	1. Task focus 2. Vigor 3. Initiative participation 4. Internalized value 5. Efficacy 6. Positive persistence

Continued

Researcher	Structural dimension
Saks (2006)	1. Job engagement 2. Organization engagement
Rich (2006)	1. Behavioral engagement 2. Cognitive engagement 3. Emotional engagement
Cha (2007)	1. Job involvement 2. Organizational identifying 3. Sense of job value
Macey and Schneider (2008)	1. psychological state engagement; 2. behavioral engagement; 3. trait engagement.
Yang (2012)	1. Job involvement: The amount of time, intelligence and energy that an employee puts in his work. 2. Job identity: The degree of employee's recognition and identification of the organization as a part of the organization. 3. The pursuit of development: the degree to which employees are willing to pursue growth and work with the organization.

The table above provides engagement dimensions divided by scholars individually. Besides scholars, many relevant organizations, consulting companies, and professional services firms are also actively involved in the study of engagement, and gave the dimensions of engagement from their own perspective. Table 2.6 summarizes the structural dimensions of engagement proposed by representative companies and firms.

Table 2.6 *Division of Dimensions of Engagement Proposed by Companies or Firms*

Company or firm	Structural dimension
Gallup (2005)	Engagement includes four dimensions: loyalty, self-confidence, pride, passion.
Hewitt (2004)	1.Saying: Employees often praise their company to colleagues, potential employees, present or potential customers. 2.Staying: Employees have a strong desire to stay with the company to continue working. 3.Striving: Employees are not only dedicated to their daily work, but also are willing to pay extra time and effort to be able to help companies achieve their goals and success.
Towers Perrin (2003)	1.Rational engagement: Employees are willing to work hard to help companies succeed through self-motivation and job involvement. It is because that employees recognize that work can bring many benefits to their own, including the accumulation of money, the upgrading of vocational skills and personal development opportunities. 2.Emotional engagement: Employees put a lot of emotion in the work, pay close attention to the company's future direction of development, due to employees engaged in their work attention, love and identifying.
Hay Group (2009)	1.Employee commitment: is an emotional bond liking the employees and the organization. It shows the willingness of the employees to stay in the organization; 2.Discretionary effort: means that employees are willing to do extra work for organization development.

Continued

Company or firm	Structural dimension
DDI (Development Dimensions International, 2005)	1 Personal value 2. Work focus 3. Interpersonal support

From the tables above, it could be said that different researchers and companies have differentiated the dimensions of engagement from different perspectives. However, there are still some consensuses among their division of dimensions. Firstly, they all considered that work engagement is multi-dimensional variable, and division of three-dimension of engagement is becoming more common. Secondly, the division of engagement dimensions by many researchers and companies is linked to three factors: physical, cognitive, and emotional. For instance, Kahn (1990) presented the concept of engagement for the first time and pointed out that the performance was at three levels: physical, cognitive, and emotional. However, he did not give operational and practical accuracy on engagement, but only stayed in the stage of conceptual research. Netherlandish psychologist Schaufeli (2002) inherited Kahn's theory and developed three dimensions: physiological dimension (vigor), emotional dimension (dedication) and cognitive dimension (absorption). Although other scholars and companies have also studied and developed different dimensions and scales, Schaufeli's dimensionality has been highly recognized and accepted in academia. UWES (Utrecht Work Engagement Scale) be based on this dimension (Schaufeli, 2002, 2009) has been validated in many countries (Zhang, 2016). Chinese scholars such as Zhang (2013) and Wang (2014) adopted this dimension division in their recent research.

Mills (2011) found that perseverance is a new dimension in some samples. Extremera (2012) pointed out that the fourth dimension is a personal accomplishment. However, the above four dimensions are only validated in a small number of studies and are not recognized by most scholars (Zhang, 2016).

In summary, work engagement includes vigor, dedication, and absorption which have been basically recognized by the academic community, and UWES based on three-dimension is also used by most scholars (Zhang, 2016). Administrative staff in universities are a special group of educators, vigor is their initiative and willingness in work, as well as psychological capacity and toughness and other psychological states when facing difficulties; dedication is the mental state and action when they achieve self - worth at work, show enthusiasm, inspiration and pride; absorption is the behavior that is absorbed in their work and is not easily disturbed by the outside world. Therefore, this study also uses these three dimensions to measure engagement of grassroots administrative staff: vigor, dedication, and absorption (Schaufeli, 2013; Schaufeli et al., 2002; Schaufeli and Bakker, 2004; Wang, 2014; Wickramasinghe, Dissanayake and Abeywardena, 2018; Zhang, 2016; Zhang and Gan, 2005).

2.5 Underlying Theories and Theoretical Framework

This section discusses related theories that underlie the present study. Overall, ERG theory, JD-R theory, psychological contract theory, self-determination theory, reciprocity norm, attribution theory, and social exchange theory are used to reveal possible relations in this study. The theoretical framework is presented below(Figure 2.1).

CHAPTER TWO : LITERATURE REVIEW

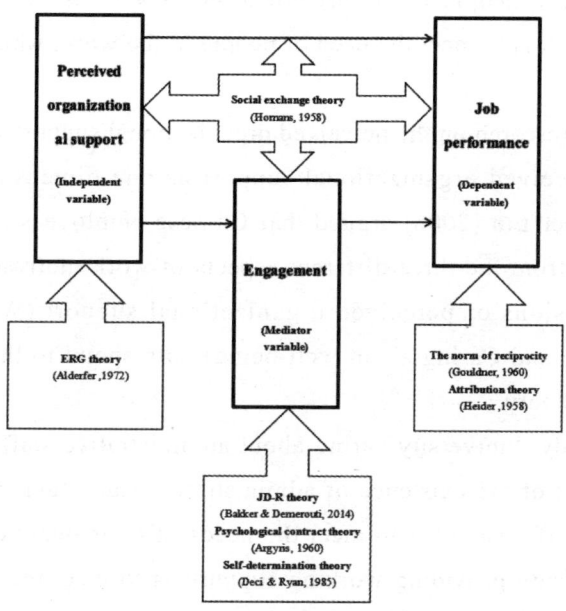

Figure 2.1. Theoretical Framework of the Study

2.5.1 ERG theory (Alderfer, 1972)

ERG theory is the underlying theory of dimensions of perceiving organizational support. ERG theory was proposed by an American psychologist Alderfer (1972) who developed the theory of Maslow's hierarchy of needs. Alderfer categorized Maslow's lower order needs, namely, physiological and safety, into the existing category. He classified the middle-level needs which are interpersonal love and esteem into his relatedness category. The Growth category contained self-actualization and self-esteem needs (Alderfer, 1969). Therefore, Maslow's hierarchy of needs theory is further developed by categorizing the hierarchy into existence, relatedness and growth which is derived from Alderfer's ERG theory. Existence means the needs of human physiology and material desires. In the life of an organization, this demand is performed by salary, welfare, work benefits, work environment. The Relatedness refers to the emotional communication and interaction between people in the organization, as well as being respected and recognized. Growth is to meet the need of people in the work, which contributes to personal growth.

In the early research on the perceived organizational support, western scholars usually take perceived organizational support as one dimension, whereas the Chinese researcher Lin (2006) argued that Chinese employees are supported by the organization from the three different aspects of work motivation to perceive. His three dimensions of perceived organizational support (Working support, Identifying value and Caring about well-being) correspond to the three needs of Alderfer's ERG theory.

For this study, 'university caring about administrative staff's well-being' is to meet the needs of the existence of administrative staff, 'university identifying administrative staff's value' is to meet the needs of relatedness of administrative staff, and 'university providing working support' is to meet the needs of growth of administrative staff. When these three dimensions of organizational support are perceived by employees and to meet their needs of ERG, the employees' mood (work engagement) and behavior (job performance) may be motivated. It can be seen that ERG theory has a good explanation for perceiving organizational support and the dimensionality of this study.

2.5.2 JD-R Theory, Psychological Contract Theory and Self-Determination Theory

JD-R theory, psychological contract theory and self-determination theory are used to explain the variable of work engagement in this study.

1. JD-R theory (Demerouti, Bakker, Nachreiner and Schaufeli, 2001)

According to Holland, Cooper and Sheehan (2016), JD-R model (demands-resources model) (Demerouti et al., 2001) has been widely used to elaborate on the work engagement. JD-R theory (Bakker and Demerouti, 2014, 2017) is developed from the JD-R model, and it is one of the most-often used theories to explain work engagement. This study uses the JD-R theory as evidence to show that engagement may play a mediating role. JD-R theory proposes that a combination of job characteristics and personal resources predicts job performance through employee work engagement. Accordingly, engagement is most likely to happen when employees are confronted with high challenges, and have sufficient job and personal resources available to deal with these challenges (e.g., Bakker and Sanz-Vergel, 2013).

Although different jobs cause different factors of job stress and job burnout, they can be classified into two types: job demands and job resources (Demerouti et al., 2001). Job demands refer to the special requirements of the job or task for employees and organizations such as role conflicts, emotional labor, work stress, etc., which are required to be achieved through employees' physical and psychological tolerance and resistance, resulting in burnout. It also affects the physical and mental health of employees negatively, and these health problems lead to a decline in employee's job performance. (Bakker and Demerouti, 2014, 2017). On the other hand, job resources also include physical, psychological, organizational, and social resources (such as support, harmony, autonomy and feedback) which help to reduce the impact of job demands and employees' strain and burnout, which in turn will enhance engagement, and then lead to positive outcomes, that is, job performance (Schaufeli, 2014).

Under the conditions of job demands and resources, different response processes will be triggered separately. One is the 'health erosion process', which reflects that due to the unreasonable work design, excessive workload and emotional labor requirements are generated in specific job positions, which continuously consumes the energy and physical strength of employees, which may lead to burnout, and then produce health problems (Demerouti et al., 2001). The other is the 'motivational process' which shows that job resources have both intrinsic and extrinsic incentives. That is, sufficient job resources are conducive to promoting employees engagement, and then possibly achieving high performance (Demerouti et al., 2001).

For this study, organizational support is considered present at the organization providing great job resources and reducing job demands, which can energize employees and foster engagement, which, in turn, yields positive outcomes such as high level of performance.

2. Psychological Contract Theory (Chris Argyris, 1960)

In this study, work engagement is also associated with the theory of Psychological Contract (Chris Argyris, 1960). Chris Argyris (1960) proposed a 'psychological work contract' when studying the relationship between workers and foremen. Levinson (1965) argued that the psychological contract is the sum of the different expectations of the inherent and unspecified differences between the organization and the employees. Kotter (1973) argued that a psychological contract is an implicit agreement between an individual and an organization; this agreement contains the content that each one wishes to pay and obtain from the other one. Schein (1992) believed that a psychological contract is a kind of coordination between the individual's willingness to dedicate and the organization's desire to obtain, and the organization's offer for personal expectations. Although it is not a tangible contract, it does play a role as a tangible contract.

The psychological contract is the mutual understanding and expectation of mutual responsibility and obligation, including employee psychological contract and organizational psychological contract (Luo, 2014). From a certain level, the intrinsic meaning of employee engagement means the establishment of a psychological contract between the organization and employees based on exchange. The concept of employee psychological contract means that both sides need to consider the effectiveness of their own commitments and the corresponding responsibility to be borne in exploring the relationship between the staff and the organization, including the responsibility of the staff for the organization and the responsibility of the organization for the staff (Luo, 2014). The researchers have reached a consensus in this field, that is, the relationship between the organization and the staff cannot achieve equality, as the former plays a decisive role in guiding the latter, and the latter plays a role in implementing and is supervised. The analysis should be carried out according to this criterion, in order to achieve the effective allocation of the responsibility of both sides (Rousseau, 1995). According to the research of Rousseau (1995), the organization's responsibility to employees should come first followed by the employees' responsibility for the organization, and employees' compensation from the organization corresponds to their contribution to the organization.

As the discussion above attests, it could be said that only when employees feel the attention and support from the organization, employees will continue to stay in the organization, and make more contributions and efforts to the organization, holding that they have an obligation to be more and more loyalty to the organization. The organization can increase employee engagement by helping employees maintain and get more resources. When employees perceive positively how the organization treats them, they will judge their attitude towards the organization through the induction of consciousness (Shore and Tetrick, 1991). When employees' needs are met, employees have a more positive perception and belief on the organization, while positive beliefs make it easier for employees to seek for a balance between their own contribution to the organization and organizational support (Shore and Wayne, 1993). Hence, work engagement is defined as a positive, fulfilling, work-related state of mind and behavior which is characterized by vigor, dedication, and absorption (Schaufeli, 2002). When grassroots administrative staff perceives university's support for them positively, they will build a psychological contract and feel an obligation to repay to the university, then form a positive, fulfilling, work-related state of mind and behavior. It can be said that the theory of psychological contract explains the work engagement and also reveals the hidden logical relationship between work engagement and perceived organizational support.

3. Self-Determination Theory (Deci and Ryan, 1985)

Self-determination theory is the motivational process theory about human determination behavior proposed by American psychologist Deci and Ryan (1985). It also can be uses to elaborate on the work engagement in this study. The theory takes the inner motivation as the starting point and studies the causal path of the influence of the environment on the individual's behavior, which has important guiding value for the incentive and change of the individual behavior (Zhang, Zhang and Song, 2011).

The theory of self-determination is based on the theory of organic dialectics. It holds that the social environment can enhance human internal motivation by supporting the satisfaction of the three basic psychological needs of autonomy, competence, and relatedness, so that the potential of individuals can be exploited to generate work engagement (Deci, 1975). Environmental factors play a role in promoting or hindering individual behavior, and organizations can intervene in the internal motivations of individuals through external environmental factors (Deci and Ryan, 1980). The three basic needs of 'autonomy, relatedness, and competence' are important factors that drive their enthusiasm which is vigor, dedication and absorption. When the social environment and the individual's internal resources can satisfy the basic psychological needs of the individual, the individual will work driven by the inherent motivation to create output actively. When the individual's basic psychological needs are hindered, the individual's positive behavior will be weakened, and even tend to adopt negative behavior. Organizations can increase human internal motivation through environmental factors that support these three basic psychological needs (Deci and Ryan, 2000). Therefore, it can be deduced that when the external factors provided by the organization can support the three basic psychological needs (autonomy, relatedness and competence) of employees, it can enhance the internal motivation, namely, work engagement (vigor, dedication and absorption) of employees to take positive action, thus stimulating the potential and promoting them to produce better job performance. Therefore, self-determination theory also can be used to elaborate on the work engagement in this study.

2.5.3 The Norm of Reciprocity and Attribution Theory

In this study, the norm of reciprocity and attribution theory is employed to explain the variable of job performance.

1. The norm of reciprocity (Gouldner, 1960)

The norm of reciprocity can be used to explain why the job performance of employees is closely related to perceived organizational support. A reciprocity norm refers to a kind of generally accepted guideline for the exchange of parties, that is, when one party provides assistance or resources for the other party, the other party is obliged to repay to those who help themselves (Gouldner, 1960). In another word, when a person treats another one well, the norm of reciprocity asks and obliges the return of favorable treatment (Eisenberger, Armeli, Rexwinkel, Lynch and Rhoades, 2001; Gouldner, 1960). Gouldner (1960), who first proposed the norm of reciprocity in his article "The Norm of Reciprocity: A Preliminary Statement", pointed out that the norm of reciprocity makes the social system more stable, it exists in all kinds of relationship between human and organizations, and applies universally to all cultures. Some scholars argued that the benefits exchanged in the norm of reciprocity should involve many different resources, such as personal resources including money, documents, services, and socioemotional resources including respect, approval and liking (e.g., Foa and Foa, 1974; Bastson, 1993). The increase of the assistance and help to a recipient can be used to increase the aid returned from the recipient and the liking for the donor (Brittingham and Kaiser, 1983; Eisenberger, Cotterell and Marvel, 1987). Therefore, the obligation to repay benefits can help enhance interpersonal relationship according to the norm of reciprocity.

The norm of reciprocity can be applied to the employer-employee relationship and organization-employee relationship. Employees must recompense the advantageous treatment they have received from the organization based on the norm of reciprocity (Porter and Steers, 1982; Wayne, Shore and Liden, 1997). In order to meet the obligations, employees have to maintain a positive self-image of repaying debts, avoid violations of reciprocity norms, and then can get beneficial treatment from their working organization (Eisenberger, et.al., 2001). Therefore, employees are motivated to compensate for favorable treatment by working in ways valued by the organization.

The positive relationships that have been found many times between perceived organizational support and job performance are attributed to feeling obligation owing to the reciprocity norm. Based on the norm of reciprocity, perceived organizational support can induce employees to feel an obligation to help organizations develop and achieve their goals of job performance (Eisenberger, et.al., 2001). Employees may repay such indebtedness through greater job performance and efforts to help the organization reach its objectives (Eisenberger et al., 1986). Therefore, in this study, the norm of reciprocity can be used to explain how administrative staff perceives their university's commitment to them through the support resources the university provides is linked with how administrative staff performs in their work. That means, the level of the university's support for administrative staff influences the level of job performance of the administrative staff provides back to the university. The norm of reciprocity indicates that administrative staff can feel obligated to repay the university's favorable treatment by good job performance (Eisenberger et al., 2004). Therefore, it could be said that the norm of reciprocity can be used to explain why the job performance of employees is closely related to perceived organizational support.

2. Attribution Theory (Heider, 1958)

Attribution theory is one of the social cognitive theories that explain the causes of people's behavior or performance. It explores what information is gathered and how it is combined to form a causal judgment (Fiske, and Taylor, 1991). For example, if someone is angry, it is because he or she has a bad temper or because something bad happened (Graham, 2014). In this study, attribution theory can be used to explain that job performance is attributed to perceived organizational support and work engagement.

There are many different attribution theories proposed by different researchers from a different perspective such as Heider's (1958) attribution theory, Jones and Davis (1965) correspondent inference theory, and Kelley's (1967) covariation model. In 1958, Heider in his book *The Psychology of Interpersonal Relations* firstly put forward the concept of attribution theory from the perspective of naive psychology. Thus, he considers the founder of attribution theory. In his study, Heider (1967) pointed out that people's performance is related to internal attribution and external attribution, which also can be called dispositional attribution and situational attribution. Internal attribution refers to the factors that exist in the people themselves, such as needs, emotions, interests, attitudes, enthusiasm, beliefs, efforts, etc. External causes refer to factors surrounding the people's environment such as expectations of other people, rewards, remuneration, penalties, instructions, orders, the weather is good or bad and so on (Heider, 1958). In other words, it can be considered that a person' performance can be attributed to their own or environment. Applying the theory of attribution to the management work reveals that when the employee's performance is not good, the manager should analyze which factors affect the employee's performance, internal attribution or external attribution. Then can help improve the employee's work performance (Shi, 2009).

In connection with this study, work engagement can be viewed as an internal factor, namely vigor, dedication and absorption, whereas organizational support can be viewed as an external factor, namely working support, identifying value and caring about well-being. Therefore, Heider's attribution theory (1958) can be used to explain the variable of job performance and its relationship with perceived organizational support and its relationship with work engagement in this study. It can be considered that job performance of grassroots administrative staff in universities is linked with not only external attribution, but also with internal attribution. Organizational support belongs to external attribution, whereas work engagement belongs to internal attribution. In order to improve job performance, both organizational support and work engagement should be improved.

Heider (1958) also pointed out that people often use the principle of covariance when doing attribution. The covariation principle states that "an effect is attributed to one of its possible causes with which, over time, it covaries" (Kelley, 1973, p. 108). That is, a certain performance is attributed to potential causes that appear at the same time. Causes of the performance can be attributed to the person (internal, such as vigor, dedication and absorption), the stimulus (external, such as working support, identifying value and caring about well-being), or some combination of these factors (Hewstone and Jaspars, 1987). Therefore, it could be said that job performance may be attributed to perceived organizational support and work engagement according to Attribution Theory (Heider, 1958).

2.5.4 Social Exchange Theory (Homans, 1958)

This study adopts the social exchange theory to elaborate on the relationship between perceived organizational support, work engagement and job performance.

Social exchange theory is a sociological theory that emerged in the United States in the 1960s, and its interpretation of individual behavior is achieved by comparing the costs and benefits of the exchange of individual and society, emphasizing the individual psychological factors in human behavior, which is also known as a behavioral social psychology theory. The theory is proposed by Homans (1958) from the perspective of economics. It is constructed by the concept of social exchange and the norm of reciprocity (Gouldner, 1960). The main content is to reflect the nature of social exchange from the essence of interpersonal relationships, including material exchange and spiritual exchange, and its core principles are embodied in 'mutual benefit'. The process of exchange is not limited to the material level, such as money, time and physical expenses, while it also has spiritual acquisition and reward, such as spiritual reward, spiritual comfort, spiritual enjoyment and social status, social identity and social fame.

Blau (1964) described social exchange as a voluntary activity or action of an individual in order to obtain the expected return. In the process of social exchange, if the results obtained by both sides that exchange is positive, then the exchange relationship between the two will continue. If there are other conditions, the smoothness of the exchange relationship may be broken, which will bring a significant blocking effect on the subsequent social interaction. Social exchange theory can explain the behavioral motives of organizations and individuals, and now many organizational theory scholars believe that social exchange theory can analyze the employment relationship in business cooperation. Organ (1988) argued that performance and loyalty are used by employees to obtain material rewards and social returns, and in the concrete process, both sides take what they need, including resources, activity and so on. The appreciation of resources can be obtained through this reciprocal action, which will strengthen each other's exchange relationship objectively. Based on the theory of social exchange, in a reciprocal relationship, the exchange of relations between the two sides is interdependent, and they suppose to take the corresponding obligations while enjoying the benefits. When one side obtains more benefits from the other side, it will reciprocate by showing favorable behavior to the other side; therefore, both sides feel the fairness of this exchange so as to maintain long-term stable exchange relationship (Luo, 2014).

In China, Wang (2015) pointed out in 'Research on Employee Total Rewards Perceptions, Engagement and Job Performance of Non-state-owned Enterprises' that social exchange theory explains the individual's behavior from the perspective of interaction between people and society. From this perspective, material remuneration and non-material remuneration are the resources provided by the organization and the organization's obligations to the employee individuals. Employees' job performance is the income obtained by the organization from the social exchange with the employees, while engagement is the implementation path for employees to achieve job performance. When the organization provides employees the appropriate remuneration and other support, employees will feel they need to work as a 'return', so they will be willing to improve self-performance in order to achieve organizational goals (Wang, 2015). This study considers university' support for administrative staff as remuneration and identification. If the administrative staff perceives the university's support, they will provide better job performance in exchange, and this exchange is achieved through work engagement.

From the above discussion, it can be seen that the theory of social exchange has laid a theoretical foundation for the relationship between perceived organizational support, work engagement and job performance.

2.6 Past Empirical Studies

2.6.1 Relationship between Perceived Organizational Support and Job Performance

A number of empirical studies on the relationship between perceived organizational support and job performance have shown that there is a positive relationship between perceived organizational support and job performance (Akgunduz and Sanli, 2017; Eisenberger et al., 2002; Kraimer, 2004; Luo, 2014; Maslach et al., 2001; Zhou and Mu, 2005). Some of these studies directly study the relationship between perceived organizational support and job performance (Akgunduz and Sanli, 2017; Maslach et al., 2001). In addition, some studies take organizational commitment, organizational identity, employee satisfaction or human resources practice as a mediator variable (Eisenberger et al., 2002; Kraimer, 2004; Luo, 2014; Zhou and Mu, 2005). However, past studies rarely associate the work engagement with the relationship between perceived organizational support and job performance.

As the earliest researcher of perceived organizational support, American researchers Eisenberger, Huntington, Hutchison and Sowa (1986) did a survey on employees from nine different industry organizations and found that perceived organizational support negatively correlated with absenteeism, and positively correlated with job performance. Since then, many American scholars began to do relevant studies. In the United States, George and Brief (1992) found that higher perceived organizational support would enable employees to show a number of additional good behaviors or actions, that is, organizational citizenship behavior. Based on the overall performance perspective, a large number of studies have proved that the enhancement of perceived organizational support is helpful to improve job performance in the United States (Armeli, Eisenberger and Fasolo, 1998; Eisenberger, Armeli and Rexwinkel, 2001; Kraimer and Wayne, 2004; Pearce and Herbik, 2004). Through a study of 308 patrols, Armeli (1998) found that social emotions play a moderating role between organizational support and police performance, which is a moderator variable. There is a positive correlation between perceived organizational support and job performance in the survey participants with strong social-emotional needs. The relationship between perceived organizational support and job performance is not significant in the survey participants with weak social-emotional needs. In a study of refinement of performance, Maslach's research showed that perceived organizational support was significantly positively correlated with task performance (Maslach et al., 2001).

Eisenberger et al.'s research (2002) is found, with 300 retail sales employees, that perceived organizational support not only played a role in improving the work of employees, but also can promote employees to take the duties outside their work, which will be conducive to improving job performance. The study of Chong et al. (2001) showed that employees in the US production industry with higher perceived organizational support hold a more positive attitude towards kanban management and have improved their performance. Riggle et al. (2009) Edmondson and Boyer (2013) used meta-analysis to find that organizational support has a positive effect on job performance.

In addition to the United States, some scholars in other countries also study the relationship between organizational support and employee performance based on the organizational cultural background of their own country (Akgunduz and Sanli, 2017; Bell et al., 2002; Joy and Krishnan, 2016; Mohamed and Ali, 2015; Truss and Soane, 2012). For example, the study of Bell et al. (2002) on service employees in Australia showed that if employees have an excellent perceived organizational support, the customer's evaluation of their quality of service is relatively high. In the UK, Alfes, Shantz, Truss and Soane (2012) selected 297 employees from service industry as participants in their investigation and found that the positive behavior of employees depends on the broader organizational climate and support. Indian assistant professors Joy and Krishnan (2016) conducted a survey of 400 employees of the information technology sector in India, and found that there is a significant relationship between perceived organizational support and high-performance work systems in India. Yilmaz and Sabahat (2016) conducted a sample survey from three cities in Turkey and used regression analysis to infer that the sense of organizational support of hotel employees has a positive predictive effect on their job embeddedness, and has a negative impact on their turnover intention. Karatepe and Aga (2016) conducted a questionnaire survey of front-line employees of banks and their supervisors in Cyprus. Through data analysis, it was found that organizational mission fulfillment and perceived organizational support could promote job performance.

Sharma and Dhar (2016) used random questionnaires to collect data from nurses in more than 300 medical institutions in Uttarakhand and analyzed the data using structural equations. It was concluded that nurses' sense of organizational support is positively related to affective commitment, and affective commitment strongly influences the performance of the nurse's work. Iranian researchers Afzali, Motahari and Hatami-Shirkouhi (2014) randomly selected nearly 300 employees from different banks in Iran for a study and found that perceived organizational support has a positive impact on organizational learning and job performance. Based on quantitative research on the survey of staff of a university in Malaysia, Mohamed and Ali (2015) concluded that perceived organizational support can improve the staff's job performance by presenting a significant relationship with perceived organizational support. Akgunduz and Sanli (2017) collected data from hotels in Turkish cities and concluded that perceived organizational support significantly positively affects employees' job embeddedness and turnover intention.

In China, there are also some scholars who are concerned about the relationship between perceived organizational support and job performance. Zhou and Mu (2005) collected a sample of 1,200 employees from 60 companies, and got the result that the influence of perceived organizational support on job performance is mostly indirect exchange through the intermediary effect of organizational commitment and job satisfaction, and only a small part is a direct exchange. Chen and Chen (2008) divided job performance into three dimensions through a survey of employees in more than ten enterprises in Wuhan: task performance, work dedication and interpersonal promotion. The study shows that perceived organizational support has a positive impact on employee performance as a whole and has a positive effect on the three dimensions of job performance. Perceived organizational support can have a positive effect on job performance through job satisfaction and emotional commitment. Zhang, Wang and Fan (2008) concluded that perceived organizational support is significantly associated with job performance through a survey of employees in state-owned enterprises, and perceived organizational support plays a regulatory role in affecting job performance in the process of human resource policy. Chen's research (2009) on knowledgeable staff in China's real estate industry has shown that perceived organizational support can effectively predict task performance and contextual performance. Qin's (2009) study on knowledge workers of financial institutions found that perceived organizational support values are significantly positively correlated with dimensions of job performance (task performance, interpersonal promotion, and work dedication). Luo (2014) selected 753 high-level talents in research universities as a survey object, and partially validated the positive predictive effect of perceived organizational support on job performance. Bi, Cai and Cai (2016) conducted a questionnaire survey on 1,218 teachers in 45 middle schools in Beijing, Shanxi, and Gansu, using covariance structure model analysis. The results showed that there is a positive correlation between organizational support and teacher performance. Liu, Chen, Chen (2019) used OLS and quantile regression analysis to find that enterprise organization support can play a role in migrant workers with different levels of worker identification, and effectively improve the level of migrant workers' engagement.

In summary, the above studies have shown that there is a direct and indirect positive relationship between perceived organizational support and job performance. The previous empirical study on the relationship between organizational support and job performance is basically targeted at employees of profitable organizations, and there are few studies for employees of nonprofit organizations, such as university employees. On the basis of previous studies findings, this study also hypothesizes that perceived organizational support is positively related to job performance of university administrative staff in China and will further determine it by a quantitative method.

2.6.2 Relationship between Perceived Organizational Support and Work Engagement

According to the review of relevant literature, there is a certain degree of positive correlation between perceived organizational support and work engagement (Caesens and Stinglhamber, 2014; Murthy, 2017; Sun and Lv, 2012). However, under the background of the popularization of higher education in China, the relationship between the perceived organizational support and work engagement of the administrative staff in newly-established universities is still uncertain and ambiguous, because it is hard to find the study which took administrative staff in Chinese newly-established universities as participants.

In the United States, Barksdale and Werner (2001) have shown that perceived organizational support can lead individuals to perform in-role behavior better. Driscoll and Randall (1999) argued that employees who are supported by the organization are more likely to consider themselves responsible for the development of the organization, which will enhance the individual's emotional commitment to the organization and reduce the willingness to leave. Eisenberger et al. (2001) surveyed 430 postal employees in the USA and concluded that employees are more dedicated when they believe that the organization will be concerned about the personal situation of the employees. Therefore, perceived organizational support gives employees a sense of responsibility, and thus they will be dedicated to working as there will be a better degree of engagement. Cathcart et al. (2004) explored the relevance between managerial control and employee engagement in the USA and the results showed that the smaller the manager's control is, the higher the employee's engagement will be.

Scholars from other countries have also shown interest in the subject. For example, in Netherland, Schaufeli and Bakker (2004) found that work resources have a significant predictive effect on job engagement. They designed three working resource factors which are feedback, management training and social support, and research findings have shown that the three factors are moderately positively correlated with engagement. In Belgium, Caesens and Stinglhamber (2014) administrated an online questionnaire to 265 employees and 112 supervisors of companies, and found that perceived organizational support is positively related to work of engagement and self-efficacy partially mediates the relationship between them. In South Africa, Rothmann and Joubert (2007) selected grassroots managers at the platinum mine as participants to study, and have also found that perceived organizational support has a significant predictive effect on these manager's degree of vigor and dedication. Meintjes and Hofmeyr (2018) found that perceived organizational support may affect employee engagement in a competitive sales environment via investigation of 125 sales representatives. In Canada, Saks (2006) carried out a survey of 102 employees who were working in different organizations in Canada, and he found that perceived organizational support, procedural justice, and other factors can significantly predict employee engagement when examining the proactive variables of employee engagement. Leiter and Laschinger (2006) also argued that the organizational environment that covers professional practice reflects a positive impact on employee engagement according to their study on nursing work life model in Canada. In India, Murthy (2017) suggested that perceived organizational support has a significant relationship with work engagement among full-time employees from nine different organizations.

In addition, some scholars (Cathcart et al., 2004; Saks, 2006) believe that other factors of organization, such as the interaction between the internal and community groups, management style and processes, organizational norms, immediate supervisor, senior management team, co-workers, work feedback, job return, job security, job roles suitability, encouraging colleagues to collaborate, superior support, fairness, interpersonal conflict and other organizational factors may have an impact on work engagement. Therefore, it can be concluded that organizational support and other relevant favorable organizational factors have positive influences on employees' work engagement in the context of Western countries in organizational culture.

In China, Yang and Liao (2009) put forward the theory of engagement degree based on the theory of social exchange, which should be established on the exchange rules of organization trust and support, employee loyalty and so on when they summarized the present situation and future prospect of employee engagement research. Chen and Zhang (2010) also believed that the establishment of perceived organizational support between enterprises and employees could significantly improve the employee's degree of engagement and analyze how to effectively restore trust to enhance the degree of engagement in response to the trust characteristics of employees and business relationships in different periods. According to a high-tech enterprise in Guangdong Province, Cao and Ning (2012) proved that perceived organizational support had played an utterly mediating role in human resource management practice and employee engagement. Through the independent questionnaire survey and regression analysis, Sun and Lv (2012) proved perceived organizational support and its predecessor variables, including procedural fairness, superior support, organization compensation and working conditions, can effectively predict the employees' degree of engagement. Hu and Liu (2016) conducted a questionnaire survey based on 215 junior high school teachers from six middle schools in Jiangsu Province, and conducted empirical research on their relationship between organizational support and job engagement. The results show that the perception of organizational support of junior high school teachers are significantly positively correlated with job engagement. Wang et al., (2017) found that extrinsic effort could reduce work engagement among Chinese female nurses, while perceived organizational support could enhance work engagement. Hospital managers should establish a supportive organizational climate to enhance Chinese female nurses' work engagement. Peng (2018) demonstrated that organizational support can significantly predict engagement by investigating employees in newly-built universities. Liu, Yang, Chu and Zhang (2019) used the Utrecht work engagement scale to investigate 536 nurses in a hospital in Harbin, and analyzed the data through SPSS 24, and concluded that organizational support has a direct effect on job engagement. It also has an indirect impact on job engagement through the psychological capital of nurses.

To sum up, both Western and Chinese scholars have validated that employees' perception of organizational support positively impacts their engagement. However, most of the respondents in the studies did not relate to the field of higher education management. Based on the findings of previous studies, this study also assumes that perceived organizational support and engagement of university administrators are positively related and it will be further examined through questionnaires.

2.6.3 Relationship between Work Engagement and Job Performance

With the emergence of the concept of engagement, the relationship between work engagement and job performance has gradually become a hotspot in the field of human resource management and consulting firms in China and abroad (Luo, 2014).

In the United States, Kahn (1990) used a qualitative method, interviewed 16 counselors and indicated that work engagement is a positive work attitude, which can affect the performance of employees more directly and significantly. The more dedicated staff will put more energy, time and effort at work, and his job performance will be higher than other employees with a low degree of engagement. Huy (1999), Rafaeli and Worline et al. (2001) also supported Kahn's findings. Kahn (1992) constructed a recursive model of psychological presence on the basis of motivation theory, further elaborated there is a positive correlation between employee engagement and job performance. Rich, Lepine and Crawford's (2010) findings of a study of 245 firefighters and their supervisors also supported their hypotheses that work engagement positively impact two job performance dimensions: task performance and organizational citizenship behavior.

However, the results of Salanova et al.'s (2005) study of employees from 58 hotels and 56 restaurants showed that work engagement cannot directly predict the job performance of employees in service units, and a service climate as a mediating variable is required to have a positive impact on job performance.

Subsequently, some companies also began to explore the relationship between work engagement and job performance, such as Gullup (2002), which is a famous research-based, global performance-management consulting company in the United States, spent more than four decades exploring the organic relationship between success of enterprises and employee engagement, and quantified a variable which is satisfaction to measure the level of engagement. A survey by Gallup in 2002 showed a triangular relationship between work engagement, satisfaction and job performance: the lower the degree of employee engagement, the worse the quality of the service for customers, and it could easily lead to loss of staff and loss of profits (Gallup, 2002). Therefore, it can be said that engagement plays a huge role in employees as a bridge between satisfaction and job performance.

There are some scholars in other countries who also conducted relevant research in addition to the ones carried out in the United States. In the Netherlands, Bakker and Bal (2010) examined a model of weekly work engagement with 54 teachers and concluded that weekly job resources can predict week-level engagement, and week-level engagement can predict week-level job performance. Then, Bakker, Vergel and Kuntze (2015) adopted quantitative diary to survey the first-year psychology students in a Dutch university. The result of the research showed that students' engagement plays a fully mediating in the relationship between their personal resources and learning performance. In Finland, Mäkikangas, Aunola, Seppälä and Hakanen (2016) conducted a survey of 1074 employees from various Finnish educational sector, and found that individual work engagement can predict team performance in the condition of increasing structural and social job resources. In Iran, Pourbarkhordari, Zhou and Pourkarimi, (2016) conducted a quantitative study of the impact of transformational leadership on employee engagement. Through questionnaires and data analysis of employees of more than 200 state-owned communications companies, they revealed that employee engagement is significantly positively correlated with job performance, and employee engagement is also mediating in the impact of change leadership on job performance.

In the United Kingdom, Wright, Carling, Lawlor and Collins (2017) also believed that engagement can positively impact on job performance according to their survey of athletes from English Championship football clubs. In India, Anitha (2014) collected data from 383 employees from small-scale organizations, through data analysis, he found that working environment and interpersonal relationship affect the employees' work engagement, meanwhile work engagement has a significant impact on job performance. Al-dalahmeh, Masa'deh, Abu Khalaf and Obeidat (2018) sought to investigate the effect of IT employees' engagement on organizational performance in the IT departments in the Jordanian banking sector. Their survey results showed that IT employee engagement positively and significantly affected job satisfaction, while job satisfaction positively and significantly affected organizational performance. This study implies that Jordanian banking IT departments in Jordanian banking should try their best to elevate IT employees' engagement and satisfaction in order to improve their performance.

Ismail, Iqbal and Nasr (2019) conducted a quantitative study in Lebanon with data from a survey of nearly 200 company employees. Their research found that employee engagement can positively impact job performance, but this impact requires creativity to have a full mediating effect between employee engagement and job performance. Ko, Lee and Koh (2017) surveyed 250 nurses working in Korean hospitals. Their study argued that job engagement has no direct effect on increasing nursing performance. However, job engagement has an indirect impact on nursing performance through mediating organizational citizenship behavior.

In China, several scholars also carried out research on the relationship between work engagement and job performance of different participants (Huo, 2008; Shao, 2007; Wen, Zhou and Wu, 2017; Yang, 2008; Zhang, 2016). Through the study of managers in middle level from high-tech enterprises, Shao (2007) proved that work engagement has a significant influence on the job performance of employees. Huo (2008) studied the intrinsic relationship between work engagement and job characteristics and job performance. Through questionnaires survey and data analysis of employees in several enterprises in the eastern and western regions of China, he found that the degree of engagement has a significant impact on the job performance of employees, and has a significant positive effect on the employees' job performance and organizational citizenship behavior. Yang (2008) used teachers in primary and secondary school as the participants of the study, proving that work engagement can directly predict job performance. Zhang (2009) conducted an empirical study on the degree of engagement of senior managers in private enterprises, and also proved the positive correlation between them. Zhang (2016) deduced that work engagement would have a positive impact on job performance through a survey of employees of 32 micro-enterprises in the catering industry in Yantai City. Wen, Zhou and Wu (2017) focused their research on the service industry. They used the vertical research method to collect the positive psychological capital, engagement and job performance data of employees three times to test the relationship between the three. The results show that the positive psychological capital of employees significantly affects their engagement and job performance, and there is also a significant positive correlation between engagement and job performance.

In view of the relationship between employee engagement and job performance, researchers have conducted empirical research from different research perspectives for different research objects, put forward a lot of inspiring research results and basically verified there was a direct positive correlation between the two variables. However, the research results of Salanova et al. (2005) showed that work engagement cannot predict the performance of employees in hotels and restaurants directly. Ko, Lee and Koh (2017) argued that job engagement has no direct effect on increasing nursing performance. It indicates that the relationship between engagement and job performance of a different group of employees may be different. This study also hypothesizes that the administrative staff's engagement is positively related to their job performance in newly-established universities in China and will further examine it through a survey.

2.6.4 Relationship between Perceived Organizational Support, Work Engagement and Job Performance

The current research on the relationship between three variables (perceived organizational support, work engagement and job performance) is still scarce, which needs to be further studied.

According to the previous study, it could be found that work engagement can mediate the relationship between organizational culture (or organizational behavior) and employee's individual performance, although such research is limited. For example, Rich, Lepine and Crawford (2010) did a study of 245 firefighters and their supervisors in the US. The result showed that work engagement mediates relationships between value congruence, perceived organizational support and two job performance dimensions: task performance and organizational citizenship behavior. In the United Kingdom, Alfes, Truss, Soane, Rees and Gatenby (2013) determined the mediating role of work engagement in the relationship between

HRM practices and job performance by a questionnaire survey of 1796 managers and employees in service-sector organizations in the United Kingdom. The result indicated that perceived HRM practices are significantly related to work on engagement, and work engagement also significantly associated with job performance and fully mediates the relationship between perceived HRM practices and task performance. Pourbarkhordari, Zhou and Pourkarimi (2016) conducted a quantitative study of the impact of transformational leadership on employee engagement. Through questionnaires and data analysis of employees of more than 200 state-owned communications companies, he revealed that employee engagement is significantly positively correlated with job performance, and employee engagement is also mediating in the impact of change leadership on job performance.

A Chinese doctor, Luo (2014), conducted a questionnaire survey of 753 university high-level talents. Through data analysis, she found that engagement plays a mediating role in the impact of organizational support on the work performance of high-level university talents. Karatepe and Aga (2016) conducted a questionnaire survey of front-line employees of banks and their supervisors in Cyprus. Through data analysis, it was found that organizational mission fulfillment and perceived organizational support could promote job performance, while job engagement fully mediates the effect of organizational mission fulfillment and perceived organizational support on job performance. Kim (2017) examined the mediation effects of work engagement by data analysis of 571 complete responses from Korean organizations. The findings showed that employee work engagement has significant partial mediating effects on the relationship between job resources and job performance. Rofcanin, Las Heras and Bakker (2017) collected questionnaires from a financial company in Mexico and found that supportive supervisor behaviors influenced work performance through subordinate work engagement. Guo, Du, Xie and Mo (2017) did a survey on 1049 employees. Their research showed that work engagement is positively related to the objective task performance, and the relationship between work engagement and objective task performance is moderated by perceived organizational support. Feng and Yang (2018) used a questionnaire to investigate 157 employees of a manufacturing enterprise in Eastern Shandong Province. The results show that work engagement plays a fully mediating role in the relationship between transactional leadership and job performance. Memon, Salleh, Nordin, Cheah, Ting and Chuah (2018) found that employee engagement can mediate the relationship between the personal-organizational fit and turnover intention through a survey on 422 oil and gas professionals. Hence, it can be seen that work engagement can play a mediating role between organizational culture (or organizational behavior) and employee's individual performance.

However, further empirical research of exploring mediation of engagement within diverse contexts and different demographic segments is needed for future study. To date, it is difficult to find research that explores the mediation of engagement between perceived organizational support and job performance. In fact, many studies take organizational commitment, organizational identity, employee satisfaction or others as a mediator variable to explore the relationship between perceived organizational support and job performance (Bell et al., 2002; Caesen and Stinglhamber, 2014; Kraimer et al., 2004).

For example, American scholars George and Brief (1992) found that organizational citizenship behavior can be promoted by perceived organizational support, which helps organizations avoid risks, construct constructive advice, gain knowledge and skills that benefit the organizations, and enhance the contextual performance of employees. Armeli, Eisenberger, Fasolo and Lynch (1998) surveyed the police patrol officers in the United States, and tried to find how the degree of social-emotional needs impact on the relationship between perceived organizational support on the job performance of police patrol officers. Then they discovered that when the individual's social-emotional needs are stronger, the organizational support's perceived values will be higher, and individuals are more likely to benefit organizations with better performance. Other studies of American scholars, such as the research of Kraimer et al. (2004) on the foreign adaptation of employees, the research of Chong et al. (2001) research on production staff, and the research of Bell et al. (2002) on corporate sales staff also showed that perceived organizational support has a high positive correlation to the job performance of employees, intermediary variables include organizational commitment, organizational identification, job satisfaction and so on.

In Belgium, Caesen and Stinglhamber (2014) surveyed 377 employees and supervisors from private companies. The findings of their study showed that self-efficacy could partially mediate the relationship between perceived organizational support and engagement of employees, and engagement can strengthen extra-role performance through increasing job satisfaction.

In China, Chen et al. (2005) opted for organizational trust and organizational self-esteem as mediators when studying the relationship between perceived organizational support and job outcomes (organizational performance, role-based performance, and organizational citizenship performance), showing that these two variables fully regulate organizational support and organizational commitment, role-based performance in the work results. In addition, the results of Chinese scholars Zhou's research (2005) on 1200 employees from 60 business in major cities, Qu's research (2006) on professional and technical staff of high-tech enterprises, Chen and Chen's research (2008) on knowledge workers with higher education background from 20 enterprises and institutions also showed that job satisfaction has a strong mediating role between perceived organizational support and job performance. The influence of perceiving organizational support on job performance is mostly 'indirect exchange' through the intermediary role of organizational commitment and job satisfaction, and only a small part is 'direct exchange'. Chen (2009) did a survey on 402 employees in Chinese companies and found that job satisfaction plays a mediating role in perceived organizational support and contextual performance. After deeply studying the relationship between perceived organizational support, work engagement and job performance among Chinese employees, Fan (2012) found that two dimensions of engagement, including identification and work value, fully mediated between organizational support and job performance, and another dimension work dedication plays a mediating role partially. Wang Hongfang, Yang (2015) revealed the transmission mechanism for the overall reward perception affects job performance through work engagement by studying employees in non-state-owned enterprises.

In general, current research on the relationship between perceived organizational support, work engagement and job performance is still scarce, especially in the field of higher education management, which needs to be further studied. In addition, through the review of the past literature, it is difficult to find a study which explored the mediating role of work engagement between perceived organizational support and job performance. On the basis of previous studies' findings and relevant theories, this study hypothesizes that university administrative staff's work engagement can mediate the relationship between their perceived organizational support and job performance. The research methodology which is used to examine this hypothesis will be further elaborated in Chapter 3.

2.7 Summary

This chapter is separated into three parts in order to assist in a preliminary understanding of what the perceived organizational support, work engagement and job performance are and how they correlate with each other. It begins with an explanation of specific definitions, including job performance, perceived organizational support, and work engagement. The second part lists and elaborates a series of theories, including ERG theory, psychological contract theory, self-determination theory, reciprocity norm, attribution theory and social exchange theory, lay a theoretical foundation and construct a theoretical framework for studying variables and exploring their relationship. The third part reviews and summarizes the previous studies related to this research, which provides empirical evidence and practical reference for studying and hypotheses of the relationship between variables. After literature review, the next chapter describes the research methodology used in this study.

CHAPTER THREE: RESEARCH METHODOLOGY

3.1 Introduction

This chapter is to present the adopted research methodology of this paper, where the research design would be explained. The choice of research methodology used in this study is outlined and discussed in this chapter. Specifically, target population, sampling techniques, sampling size, instrumentation of the survey, questionnaire design, three different measurement scales, language translation, the process of data collection, study ethics, data analysis techniques and pilot study results are explained in detail.

It is necessary to clearly and simply present the entire design flow of the study in the form of a chart, because the research process of this study is complicated and involves a lot of content. Therefore, a research flowchart is presented below to describe briefly the whole design process of the research, which especially focuses on the methodology design.

CHAPTER THREE : RESEARCH METHODOLOGY

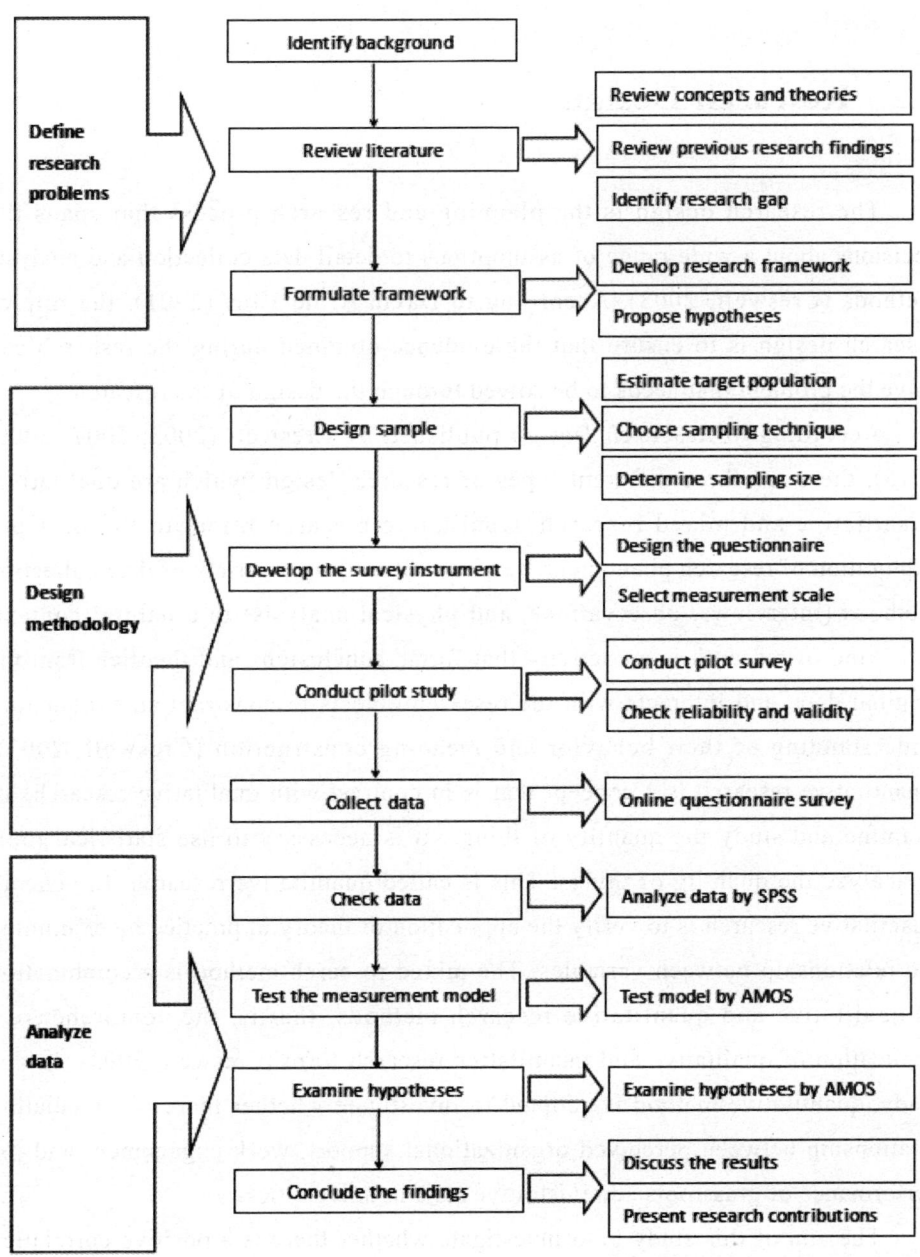

Figure 3.1. Flowchart of the Study Design

3.2 Research Design

The research design is the planning and research process that spans the decisions about a wide range of assumptions to detail data collection and analysis methods (Creswell, 2003). According to David A. de Vaus (2001), the role of research design is to ensure that the evidence obtained during the research can solve the problem that needs to be solved through the design of the research.

According to *Research Design* published by Creswell (2003, 2007, 2009, 2013), there are three different types of research design, which are qualitative, quantitative and mixed research. Qualitative research refers to the in-depth exploration of research phenomena by researchers using a variety of data collection methods (interviews, observations, and physical analysis) in a natural context. This kind of research is an activity that forms conclusions and theories from the original data, and interacts with the research objects to construct an explanatory understanding of their behavior and meaning construction (Creswell, 2003). Quantitative research is a concept that is in contrast with qualitative research. To examine and study the quantity of things, it is necessary to use statistical tools to analyze the quantity of things. This is called quantitative research. In general, quantitative research is to verify the application of theory in practice by examining the relationship between variables. The mixed research method is a combination of qualitative and quantitative research methods, that is, the comprehensive application of qualitative and quantitative research form (Creswell, 2003). In this study, quantitative method is adopted to investigate whether there is a mediating relationship between perceived organizational support, work engagement and job performance of grassroots administrative staff in universities.

The aim of this study is to investigate whether there is a positive correlation between perceived organizational support, work engagement and job performance of grassroots administrative staff in universities. The study also examines the role of work engagement as a mediator between perceived organizational support and job performance. This study is correlational in nature. The hypotheses testing in line with the purpose of the study examined the relationship to which variations in one factor correspond with variations in one or more factors based on correlation coefficient (Cronbach, 1951; Isaac and Michal, 1981). Therefore, quantitative research is adopted in this study according to the elaboration of Creswell (2003) and Williams and Monge (2001). Quantitative method is suitable when three conditions are present: 1) It is possible to establish hypotheses based on theory and to verify them; 2) Research tools can be used to measure research target objects; and 3) statistical knowledge can be used to solve research problems.

Furthermore, a self-administrated questionnaire is adopted in this study to be an effective way to collect the data. And the data analysis techniques employed by the study include normality test, descriptive statistical analysis, reliability test, validity test, and correlation analysis.

3.3 Sampling

This section elaborates three important steps, which are the target population, sampling technique, and sample size to satisfy the prerequisite for the study.

3.3.1 Target Population

According to Malhotra (2004), the target population refers to the gathering of items and components in order to provide information for conducting research.

The target population for this study is grassroots administrative staff in newly-established universities in Sichuan, China. It is generally considered that administrative staff in newly-established universities in China can be divided into three levels: senior (decision-making level), middle (management level), grassroots (operational level) (Ding, 2009; Xu, 2007). As illustrated in Table 1.1 in Chapter 1, Senior administrative staff refers to Ting and Deputy Ting at 3 or 4 grade, and they are the leaders of the university. Middle-level administrative staff refers to the Chu and Deputy Chu at 5 or 6 grade, and they are the leaders of a college or department of a university. Grassroots administrative staff refers to the Ke and

Deputy Ke and staff at the 7-10 grades. They are engaged in academic affairs, research management, human resources management, financial management, infrastructure, library management, logistics services, and other management affairs in different departments of the university.

Currently, there are 22 newly-established universities in Sichuan Province. Table 3.1 below shows the main details about 22 newly-established universities in Sichuan Province which are queried and summarized from Information Inquiry System of Chinese Universities (http://www.gx211.com/gxmd/gx-sc.html).

Table 3.1 *Main Details of Newly-established Universities in Sichuan, China*

University	Public or Private	Location	department in charge	Date of establishment
University A	Public	Neijiang	Sichuan Provincial Government	2000
University B	Public	Leshan	Sichuan Provincial Government	2000
University C	Public	Yibin	Sichuan Provincial Government	2001
University D	Public	Panzhihua	Sichuan Provincial Government	2001
University E	Public	Mianyang	Sichuan Provincial Government	2002
University F	Public	Chengdu	Sichuan Provincial Government and Chengdu Government	2003
University G	Public	Xichang	Sichuan Provincial Government	2003
University H	Public	Chengdu	Sichuan Provincial Government	2004

Continued

University	Public or Private	Location	department in charge	Date of establishment
University I	Public	Dazhou	Sichuan Provincial Government	2006
University J	Public	Luzhou	Sichuan Provincial Government and Sichuan Public Security Department	2006
University K	Public	Kangding	Sichuan Provincial Government	2009
University L	Public	Chengdu	Sichuan Provincial Government	2012
University M	Public	Chengdu	Sichuan Provincial Government	2012
University N	Public	Chengdu	Sichuan Provincial Government	2013
University O	Public	Aba	Sichuan Provincial Government	2016
University P	Private	Chengdu	Education Department of Sichuan	2011
University Q	Private	Chengdu	Education Department of Sichuan	2013
University R	Private	Deyang	Education Department of Sichuan	2014
University S	Private	Chengdu	Education Department of Sichuan	2014
University T	Private	Chengdu	Education Department of Sichuan	2014

Continued

University	Public or Private	Location	department in charge	Date of establishment
University U	Private	Mianyang	Education Department of Sichuan	2014
University V	Private	Chengdu	Education Department of Sichuan	2016

Note: The real names of all newly-established universities are replaced by letters.

In order to reasonably identify the sample size, it is necessary to calculate the number of the target population. The calculation of the target population of the study was divided into two steps.

The first step was to inquire into the staff population of newly-established universities in Sichuan. The researcher visited the official website of each newly-established university, and contacted several universities' human resource departments in order to obtain the data on the approximate population of faculty and administrative staff of newly-established universities in Sichuan.

The second step was to calculate the number of grassroots administrative staff in the newly-established universities. Grassroots administrative staff is part of the administrative staff, but it is difficult to directly identify their specific number in each university. According to *Implementation Opinions on the Post Setting Management of Institutions in Sichuan Province*. (Sichuan Provincial Government, 2008) issued by Sichuan government, the number of Ke post and the following administrative post (Grades 7—10) must account for about two-thirds of the total number of administrative posts in the university. That is to say, grassroots administrative staff is supposed to occupy two-thirds approximately of the total number of administrative staff in each newly-established universities.

According to this criterion, the researcher calculated the population of the grassroots administrative staff in each newly-established university based on the number of administrative staff which was found out in the first step. More details are shown in Table 3.2 below.

Table 3.2 *The Number of Grassroots Administrative Staff in Newly-Established Universities in Sichuan*

University	Total number of staff	The number of administrative staff	Estimated number of grassroots administrative staff
University A	1233	359	239
University B	1200	368	245
University C	1010	235	157
University D	1039	201	134
University E	1181	262	175
University F	1205	362	241
University G	970	179	119
University H	737	221	147
University I	1100	327	218
University J	480	144	96
University K	533	191	127
University L	857	257	171
University M	980	294	196
University N	602	140	93
University O	579	174	116
University P	774	232	155
University Q	1000	298	199
University R	946	284	189
University S	580	173	115
University T	1119	336	224
University U	801	224	150

Continued

University	Total number of staff	The number of administrative staff	Estimated number of grassroots administrative staff
University V	704	197	131
Total number	19630	5458	3637

Note: The real names of all newly-established universities are replaced by letters.

3.3.2 Sampling Techniques

According to Creswell (2003) and Sekaran (2016), sampling consists of selecting the right individuals or objects for the study. Saunders et al. (2009) stressed that the sampling provides a range of methods allow reducing the amount of data that we are obliged to collect by considering only data from sub-group rather than all possible cases. It means the researcher would obtain the data from the sample in order to examine the situation or the purpose of the study rather than collecting the data from the entire subject. The purpose of sampling is to decrease the time and cost of the data collection process (Hair et al., 2006).

There are two broad categories of sampling techniques, namely, non-probability sampling and probability sampling. Non-probability sampling consists of snowball sampling, judgmental sampling, quota sampling, and convenience sampling. Probability sampling involves systematic sampling, cluster sampling, simple random sampling, and multistage sampling (Lance and Hattori, 2016). The sampling is based on the fact that every member of a population has a known and equal chance of being selected. Probability sampling has a sound statistical theory basis and can be explained by probability theory. It is an objective and scientific sampling technique. It is a mathematically specialized term and is based on the randomness theory to extract the same number of samples of the population as the study object. The probability that each sample is sampled is equal, thus ensuring that the sample is not doped with so-called artificial factors. Probability sampling is the basic sampling technique in quantitative research (Fowler, 2014).

In this study, cluster sampling is adopted. It is done by grouping the elements in the population into a number of groups that do not cross each other and do not overlap with each other; then the samples are taken in groups (Lance and Hattori, 2016). Cluster sampling is often used in quantitative research where the total population is divided into several groups (called clusters), and a simple random sample of the clusters is selected. The elements in each cluster are then sampled (Kerry and Bland, 1998). If all elements in selected sampled groups are sampled, then this is referred to as a one-stage cluster sampling plan. If the cluster samples in the first stage are selected and then followed by the selection of the element samples from each sample cluster, a two-stage clustering sample is obtained, which is a simple multi-stage sample case referred to as a two-stage cluster sampling plan (Ahmed, 2009). That is to say, the researcher divides the sample population into N groups, then randomly selects several groups from N groups, and randomly selects individuals in chosen groups. More specifically, the first step is to determine the criteria for grouping. Secondly, according to the sample size, the number of groups that should be drawn was determined and randomly selected. Thirdly, a simple random sampling method was used to select a certain number of sample populations from the selected clusters.

In this study, samples were chosen by two-stage cluster random sampling. To be specific, the study is to measure the perceived organizational support, work engagement and job performance among grassroots administrative staff in newly-established universities, but it is impossible and difficult to visit each grassroots administrative staff to collect data. In fact, the target population of the study can be divided into 22 pre-existing groups, namely, 22 newly-established universities. Therefore, the appropriate way for sampling in this study is to randomly select several universities (clusters) and randomly survey the grassroots administrative staff in those universities. Each newly-established university in Sichuan and each grassroots administrative staff would have an equal opportunity of being selected. More details on cluster sampling process are shown in Figure 3.2.

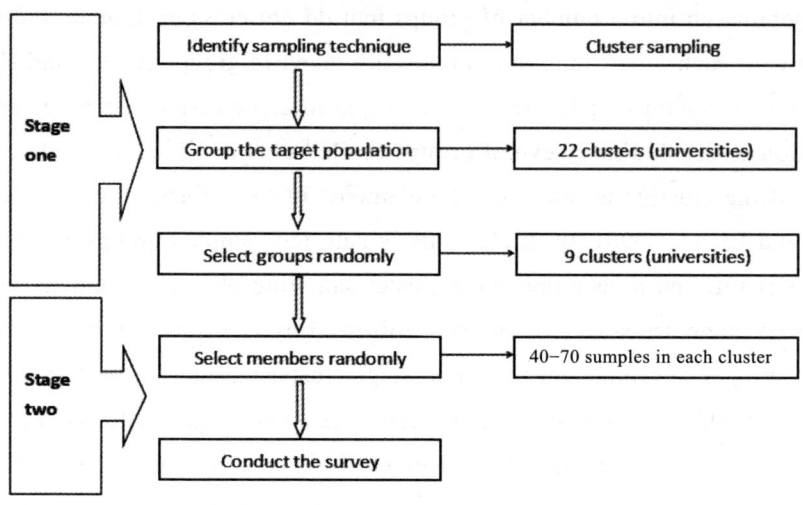

Figure 3.2. Flowchart of Sampling

3.3.3 Sampling Size

Sample size refers to the number of units contained in a sample, usually expressed by the letter N, which is a fundamental concept in research design. The size of the sample is directly related to the accuracy of the research results (Creswell, 2003). In the investigation, the determination of the sample size is very important. The sample size is generally determined by the population of the study target. If the sample size is too large, it will cause a great waste of manpower, material resources and financial resources; if the sample size is too small, it may cause the survey results to deviate from the actual situation, affecting the authenticity of the survey. (Bartlett, Kotrlik and Higgins, 2001).

Schumacker and Lomax (1996) found that the numbers of samples of most of the research which adopted SEM (structural equation model) for data analysis are in the range of 200–500. Wu (2012) argued that the number of medium-sized sampling must be greater than 200; if the number of samples reaches 200 or more, the results of the analysis are relatively stable. Muller and Pasour (1997) argued that the number of samples analyzed by structural equation model is at least 100 and 200. If the number of samples is estimated from the number of variables observed in the model, the ratio of the number of samples to the number of observed variables is at least 10 : 1 to 15 : 1. Hinkle and Oliver (1983) make it clear that the research findings from the larger sampling size will be more credible than the small sampling size when other conditions remain constant. Therefore, the selection of a larger sampling size is appropriate and necessary. In this study, the researcher also tries to make the research sampling size larger.

There are several formulas for calculating the required sample size based on whether the data collected is to be a categorical or quantitative in nature. However, Krejcie and Morgan (1970) have already constructed a table which can help researchers avoid the formulas altogether.

Table 3.3 *Table for determining sample size of knowing population (Krejcie and Morgan, 1970)*

N	S	N	S	N	S	N	S	N	S
10	10	100	80	280	162	800	260	2800	338
15	14	110	86	290	165	850	265	3000	341
20	19	120	92	300	169	900	269	3500	346
25	24	130	97	320	175	950	274	4000	351
30	28	140	103	340	181	1000	278	4500	354
35	32	150	108	360	186	1100	285	5000	357
40	36	160	113	380	191	1200	291	6000	361
45	40	170	118	400	196	1300	297	7000	364
50	44	180	123	420	201	1400	302	8000	367
55	48	190	127	440	205	1500	306	9000	368
60	52	200	132	460	210	1600	310	10000	370
65	56	210	136	480	214	1700	313	15000	375
70	59	220	140	500	217	1800	317	20000	377
75	63	230	144	550	226	1900	320	30000	379

Continued

N	S	N	S	N	S	N	S	N	S
80	66	240	148	600	234	2000	322	40000	380
85	70	250	152	650	242	2200	327	50000	381
90	73	260	155	700	248	2400	331	75000	382
95	76	270	159	750	254	2600	335	100000	384

Note: N is Population Size; S is Sample Size

The above table helps researchers avoid using formulas. In this research, the target population is about 3637 grassroots administrative staff in newly-established universities. The researcher uses this table to determine the appropriate sample size for the study, and decides that 351 should be sufficient for investigation according to Table 3.2 and Table 3.3 which are presented in Chapter 2. Moreover, according to a suggestion by Hinkle and Oliver (1983) that a larger sampling size is more reliable, the researcher decides to use a sample size of 400 for this study.

3.4 Instrumentation

A survey allows the researchers to gather ideas and recommendations from several individuals at a subjective stage to confirm whether there are any opinion and advice to the target population (Creswell, 2003; Sekaran, 2003). Surveys can be divided into two broad categories: the questionnaire and the interview. The questionnaire is research instrumentation making up of a series of questions for the purpose of gathering information from respondents (Gault, 1907). The questionnaire survey saves time, money and manpower, and it is convenient for statistical processing and analysis. Moreover, the electronic questionnaire developed in recent years can overcome some of the shortcomings of the traditional paper questionnaire and makes it more convenient and easy for quantitative research (Jing, Gao and Liu, 2008). Therefore, the questionnaire survey is adopted in the study.

3.4.1 Questionnaire Design

The design of the main body of the questionnaire will directly influence the value of the entire investigation (Zheng, 2014). In designing the questionnaire, this research has taken the research purpose, related literature researches and questionnaire structures into comprehensive consideration.

The main purpose of this survey is to measure perceived organizational support, work engagement and job performance among grassroots administrative staff in newly-established universities, hence the main body of the survey questionnaire is composed of three different measurement scales, including perceived organizational support scale by Ling et al. (2006), Utrecht work engagement scale by Schaufeli and Bakker (2004) and job performance scale by Yu (1996). It should be pointed out that these three scales were developed separately by the relevant scholars, meaning that they are independent and complete sets of scales, not extracted from a questionnaire in the past study. Since all three measurement scales have been widely used in the previous study, in the questionnaire of this study, they were maintained in their original appearance (content), without deleting or adding items. However, based on the opinions and suggestions of the experts, the way several items were expressed has been improved so that the respondents can understand the meaning of the items more accurately. The relevant improved items are summarized by a table in the pilot study.

Special attention has been paid to the following aspects:

1. Introduction, main questionnaire and personal information are the three general parts composing the survey questionnaire. The introduction is to briefly describe the purpose and contents of the survey so that the requests and acknowledgments are indispensable; otherwise the respondents may not be cooperative and supportive for they feel no sincerity of the researcher. In the content of the main questionnaire, the scales on three variables are established to provide questions. No unstructured questions are adopted, seeing that the open-ended questions will not be advantageous to improve the respondents' willingness to fill in the questionnaire (O'Cathain and Thomas, 2004), thus the investigation

adopts the structured choice question items to let the respondents make choice but do not need to write words and sentences.

2. Considering that the Likert Scale has quite higher credibility than other scales, it is widely adopted in the survey questionnaire; in addition, the five-grade scale is convenient for the respondents to discriminate the degrees of attitude (Armstrong, 1987). Therefore, Likert Scale is employed in this research. Options following each declarative sentence mean the gradually increasing consent on the forward direction, namely: 1 means strongly disagreed, 2 means disagreed, 3 means neutral, 4 means agreed and 5 means totally agreed.

3. To dispel the misgivings of the respondents in the benefit-risk balance established by the reverse questions and positive questions in the scale, all questions are positive in the scale. This is to ensure that the consistency of positive thinking of the respondents can be guaranteed and they can think about the questions carefully, maintain the smooth thought logically and consequently guarantee the high quality of the answers to the questionnaires.

4. The research questionnaires are self-administered where all questions are answered by the respondents. The self-administered questionnaire refers to the method in which the researcher sends the questionnaire to the respondents, which is read and answered by the respondents, and then collected by the researcher (Bourque and Fielder, 2003). Comparing with the Interviewer-administered questionnaires, the self-administered questionnaires have three advantages: firstly, it could save time, cost and manpower; secondly, the anonymity is helpful for the respondents to fill in the questionnaires truthfully, so as to collect the objective and true information; thirdly, it could avoid the human errors caused by the subjective thoughts of the interviewer in the interviewer-administered questionnaires (Meadows, 2003).

5. The content of this questionnaire is mainly composed of three parts, namely the introduction, basic personal information and the main part of the questionnaire. The introduction mainly introduces the purpose of the questionnaire survey; the basic personal information contains the respondents' gender, marital status, age, educational background and academic rank; the main part of the questionnaire is composed of respective questions measuring the perceived organizational support, work engagement and job performance.

Based on related research carried out by local and foreign scholars, the researcher selects the maturity scales that have been published and have been tested many times for their reliability and validity to measure the relevant variables.

3.4.2 Perceived Organizational Support Scale

This study adopts Ling et al.'s scale (2006) to measure perceived organizational support of grassroots administrative staff in newly-established universities in China. The perceived organizational support scale established by Ling et al. (2006) is more frequently adopted by the scholars in the Chinese context (Liu and Li, 2015; Luo, 2014; Ma, 2016; Zhang, 2013). This scale contains three dimensions namely the working support, identifying value and caring about well-being. Thus, it adopts in this study. In the following section, this paper makes a review of the related study and development of perceived organizational support scale.

In terms of measuring the perceived organizational support, Eisenberger and Huntington (1986) put forward the concept of perceived organizational support and formulated the perceived organizational support scale, namely the SPOS questionnaire (Survey of Perceived Organizational Support) for the first time in their academic article *Perceived Organizational Support*. This kind of questionnaire is frequently adopted in the Western countries' academic field to measure perceived organizational support; 36 items of the questionnaire in this scale have been tested among the employees of different industries and organizations, according to the result of which, this scale is of one-dimension and high credibility. Some researchers extracted items with a high load factor from the 36 items of the questionnaire of perceived organizational support and then developed them into a short questionnaire to carry out research. The core elements of these scales are the employees' two feelings for the organizations. One is whether the employee's contributions are identified and valued; the other one is whether the employee's well-being is an important concern (Liu, 2015; Luo, 2014). The perceived organizational support scale developed by McMillan (1997) is composed of two parts, namely the instrumental support and emotional support. Some scholars also adopt this scale to measure the perceived organizational support.

In the context of Chinese organization, the perceived organizational support questionnaire established by Ling et al. (2006) is more frequently adopted by the Chinese scholars at present. This questionnaire contains three dimensions, namely, working support, identifying value and caring about well-being. This questionnaire was made under the context of Chinese culture and regarded the employees' perceived organizational support as a three-dimensional psychological structural feeling. The perceived organizational support of multi-dimensional structure has reflected the employees' work motivations, namely the material living guarantees provided by the organization, being recognized and respected in the organization and self-realization by making achievement in work. The perceived organizational support scale developed by Ling et al. contains 24 questions (Ling, Yang and Fang, 2006). This questionnaire is widely recognized and adopted in the research on Chinese employees' perceived organizational support and related research fields, and has been repeatedly proved with favorable reliability and validity. Therefore, in this research, the scale is directly employed to measure the perceived organizational support of the grassroots administrative staff in the newly-established universities. Table 3.4 below shows dimensions and items of Perceived Organizational Support Scale by Ling et al. (2006).

Table 3.4 *Perceived Organizational Support Scale by Ling et al. (2006)*

Dimensions	Items
Working Support	1. I can be noticed by the superiors when I am working exceptionally.
	2. The organization attaches special importance to my job objectives and the concept of values.
	3. The organization does not take advantage of me during work as long as there are opportunities.
	4. I can get help from superiors and colleagues when I have problems at work.

Continued

Dimensions	Items
Working Support	5. The organization can agree with my reasonable request to change the working conditions or environments.
	6. The organization is happy to help me explore my potential at work.
	20. The organization can pay attention to my opinion at work
	21. The organization can provide me some opportunities for promotion.
	22. The organization puts me at the positions that I am most suitable for.
	24. The organization tries the best to make our work interesting.
Identifying Value	9. The organization believes it's a large loss to dismiss me.
	10. The organization believes that I will play a great role if it keeps me within the organization.
	11. The organization will employ me if I apply for the job after I have quit.
	12. The organization will never dismiss the employees arbitrarily.
	17. The organization will persuade the employees who want to quit to stay.
	18. The organization will transfer me to other positions but not dismiss me if my job cancels.
	19. The organization is proud of the achievements I have made at work.
Caring about Well-being	7. The organization can understand and forgive me for the occasional absence from work for personal reasons.
	8. The organization can reward me for the extra work I have done beyond the proper duties.
	13. The organization really cares about my living conditions.
	14. The organization can consider the salary I deserve.

Continued

Dimensions	Items
Caring about Well-being	15. The organization can happily provide help when I am in need of special help.
	16. The organization can take the well-being of the employees into consideration at the time of making a decision.
	23. The organization can consider increasing our salaries when it obtains more profits.

3.4.3 Work Engagement Scale

In this study, the Utrecht Work Engagement Scale (UWES) by a Dutch scholar, Schaufeli (2002), is used to measure the work engagement of grassroots administrative staff in newly-established universities. As UWES has been tested in reliability, validity and verified in trans-cultural stability, it has been adopted in this research (Schaufeli and Bakker, 2004; Wang, 2014; Zhang and Gan, 2005).

As the Chinese and foreign scholars, as well as the consultant firms, are not unified in the concept and structural cognition of engagement, the engagement measurement scales they adopt in the empirical study and business consultancy practice are different (Gallup, 2005; Maslach, 1997; Schaufeli, 2002). The following three are the commonly adopted: Gallup's 12 Questions to measure engagement (Q12) by Gallup (2005), Maslach Burnout Inventory General Survey (MBI) by Maslach (1997) and the UWES by Schaufeli (2002). Gallup Workplace Audit (GWA), the world's famous management consulting firm, has developed the engagement measurement scale containing an overall work satisfaction question and 12 specific questions through the qualitative and quantitative studies on the interview results of millions of employees. According to a large number of empirical studies, Q12 is a single-dimensional structure with higher validity and reliability as well as the trans-cultural stability, hence being widely recognized and applied in empirical research. However, some scholars also question the validity of the measurement. For instance, Li and Ling (2007) argued that the results measured by Q12 only represent the work satisfaction of the employees.

Maslach et al. (1997) believed that the engagement can be directly measured by MBI and evaluated by the reverse patterns of the scores on the three dimensions namely exhaustion, cynicism and professional efficacy, which means the lower scores on exhaustion and cynicism and higher scores on professional efficacy represent the higher work engagement. However, this viewpoint was questioned by Schaufeli et al. (2002) as they believed that it would be difficult to empirically investigate the relationship between work engagement and exhaustion if these two concepts are measured by the same instrument.

To independently measure the work engagement, Schaufeli et al. (2002) constructed UWES. The work engagement was measured from three aspects namely vigor, dedication and absorption with 17 questions. Soon afterward, Schaufeli and Bakker (2004) published the *UWES Preliminary Manual* to report a series of data from the psychological measurement and verification on the Utrecht scale, so as to assist and guide the subsequent researchers in selecting and using UWES. In addition, Schaufeli and Bakker (2004) developed a shortened scale with nine questions based on the original 17-question scale. It should be noted that the verification data were obtained by analyzing the trans-national and trans-industrial samples. Hence, this scale has high reference values (Wang, 2014). In China, Zhang and Gan (2005) have verified the reliability and validity of the Utrecht scale in Chinese version, according to the result of which, this scale was applicable to the research involving Chinese background. As UWES has been tested in reliability, validity and verified in trans-cultural stability, it has been adopted in this research. Table 3.5 below shows dimensions and items of the shortened version of UWES by Schaufeli et al. (2004).

Table 3.5   *Work Engagement Scale by Schaufeli et al. (2004)*

Dimensions	Items
Vigor	1. At my work, I feel bursting with energy.
	2. At my job, I feel strong and vigorous.
	3. When I get up in the morning, I feel like going to work.

Continued

Dimensions	Items
Dedication	4. I am enthusiastic about my job.
	5. My job inspires me.
	6. I am proud of the work that I do.
Absorption	7. I feel happy when I am working intensely.
	8. I immerse in my work.
	9. I get carried away when I'm working.

3.4.4 Job Performance Scale

This study utilizes job performance scale established by Yu (1996) to measure job performance of grassroots administrative staff in newly-established universities.

The division of job performance has undergone a different process, which only focused on results at the beginning, that is, task performance, and later not only focused on results, but also paid attention to processes, that is, contextual performance (Zhao, 2012). The difference between task performance and contextual performance in job performance has been widely noted by academics. Subsequent studies of scholars mostly have supported a two-dimension structure of job performance (Hou and Chen, 2011). The job performance addressed in this paper should be a comprehensive consideration of the characteristics of the administrative performance of universities, mainly to measure the performance of the results and the performance of the process. Therefore, the job performance of administrative workers in universities is divided into two dimensions: task performance and contextual performance.

In the 1980s, Darling-Hammond, Wise and Pease (1983) proposed establishing the scale from the four aspects including personal career development, human resource management policy, school development and school status to evaluate the job performance of the academic staff, which has laid the foundation for the study on the job performance of teachers. The dimensions of the job performance

CHAPTER THREE : RESEARCH METHODOLOGY

of teachers in developed countries are derived from the above four aspects. For instance, the measurement of job performance of American academic staff adopts the three-dimensional method, that is, teaching, research and service (Luo, 2014). The measurement of job performance of Chinese teachers has followed the American three-dimensional method. Fang (2006) measured the job performance of academic staff from four dimensions namely qualification, teaching, scientific research and management; Gan (2006) carried out a research on the job performance of academic staff from input, control and output; while Luo (2014) developed the teachers' job performance scale from two dimensions including teaching and scientific research. Although the administrative staff is part of the university faculty, their job contents and characteristics are greatly different from those of the academic staff. As teaching and scientific research are not their major job tasks, the teacher's job performance scale is not applicable to measure the job performance of the administrative staff. Initially, the researcher planned to adopt the job performance scale for measuring the teachers but for the aforementioned reasons, the plan was dropped.

Job performance is divided into two dimensions which are task performance and contextual performance, On the acceptance and support of these dimensions, Taiwan scholar Yu (1996) compiled the job performance scale suitable to the Chinese culture by integrating the Task Performance Questionnaire (TPQ) established by Campbell (1987) and Contextual Performance Questionnaire (CPQ) created by Motowidlo and Scotter (1994), and made necessary modification and translation (Cai, 2015; Liu, 2007; Xia, 2010). This scale has been proved with favorable reliability and validity by many Chinese scholars. A research on Chinese bank clerk by Xia (2010), a research on Chinese young civil servant by Zheng (2012) and a research on Beijing's full-time communist youth league cadres by Yu (2014) all adopted Yu's scale (1996) to measure the job performance. In this research, job performance is also divided into two dimensions namely task performance and contextual performance. Moreover, Yu's revised scale is more suitable to the Chinese cultural background, so that it has been adopted in this research. Table 3.6 below shows more details of Job Performance Scale by Yu (1996).

Table 3.6 *Job Performance Scale by Yu (1996)*

Dimensions	Items
Task Performance	1. I finish the work according to the standard operating procedures.
	2. I am familiar with standard operating procedures.
	3. I plan and arrange the schedule of the work I am responsible for.
	4. I pay attention to safety and health problems at work.
	5. I keep the working field tidy and clean.
	6. I put the tools or documents at hand in order and take things back where they were.
	7. My average work efficiency is high.
	8. I am capable of completing all the tasks required by the organization.
Contextual Performance	9. I cooperate with others well in the team.
	10. I persist in overcoming obstacles to complete a task.
	11. I volunteer for additional responsibilities.
	12. I follow standard operating procedures and avoid unauthorized shortcuts.
	13. I look for challenging assignments.
	14. I offer to help others accomplish their work.
	15. I pay close attention to important details.
	16. I defend the supervisor's decisions.
	17. I render proper business courtesy.
	18. I support and encourage a coworker with a problem.
	19. I take the initiative to solve a work task.
	20. I exercise personal discipline and self-control.
	21. I tackle a difficult work assignment enthusiastically.
	22. I voluntarily do more than the job requires helping others or contributing to organizational effectiveness.

Continued

Dimensions	Items
Contextual Performance	23. Overall, I would like to consider the organization and take the initiative to help my coworkers.

3.4.5　Language Translation

In designing a questionnaire, language translation must be considered (Mckay et al., 1996). The questionnaire should be translated into different language versions so that the study can be understood by people using different languages. There are three scales in the questionnaire: the first and third scales, namely, perceived organizational support scale and job performance scale were established by Chinese scholars, thus they do not need to be translated into Chinese. The second scale, namely, UWES is quite well-known and has been widely adopted all over the world. Its preliminary manual has already provided 12 different language versions including Chinese. Therefore, it does not need to translates into Chinese either. However, the researcher translated perceived organizational support scale and job performance scale into English in order to make relevant people who are interested in this study understand the questionnaire. This process of translation was done using the back translation method because the back translation is regarded as the best practice when it comes to questionnaire design (Mckay et al., 1996). The researcher asked two English language experts from Yibin University to translate the Chinese version into English and then re-translate the English version into Chinese. Repeated comparisons and modifications were done to ensure the accuracy of the translation.

3.5　Data Collection

Primary data are the elementary sources for directing the research. According to Zikmund et al. (2010), primary data are described as data that are assembled for the research purpose of the existing situation whereby the events are happening.

There are several approaches to gather primary data. One of the approaches is a questionnaire which has already been adopted broadly by most researchers and could help to collect the data effectively. Therefore, in this study, the researcher chooses the online questionnaire as a method of collecting the primary data as it can increase the simplicity and reliability of the information for the research.

3.5.1 Online Questionnaire

With scientific and technological progress, network development is also changing rapidly. Compared with the traditional paper-based questionnaire, the online questionnaire survey has become a more convenient and popular data-collection method (Couper, 2012; He, 2016). It is mainly for the following three reasons that the current research has adopted the online questionnaire for data collection:

First is to avoid the social desirability response bias. In any society, there will be publicly recognized moral standards and codes of conduct. If questions in the questionnaire have touched these standard norms, the respondents are likely to turn on the self-protection or self-service motivation, so that they will answer the questions from the perspective of social desirability and expectation instead of showing their honest opinions—this is the so-called social desirability response bias (Chen, Xu, Fan, 2012; Crowne, Marlowe, 1960). Paulhus (1991) believed that answers twisted to meet the social desirability tend to be two kinds of representation patterns. One is the authentic yet exaggerated positive self-expression, the other is the impression management, which means to intentionally change one's own opinions or behaviors to please others. If the researcher adopts the survey method of paper-based questionnaire, the researcher will entrust the human resource departments of newly-established universities to give out some questionnaires to the respondents who are grassroots administrative staff. Although the respondents fill in the questionnaire anonymously, considering that their questionnaires will be submitted to the human resource department, there might be social desirability response bias when they are filling in the questionnaires.

After reviewing and analyzing almost 200 research reports, Dwight et al. (2000) pointed out that the score of impression management test in the way of computer-filling was lower than in the way of paper-pencil-filling, so that the way of computer-filling could better reflect the honest opinions of the respondents. If the online questionnaires are adopted in the survey, after the respondents have completed and submitted the questionnaires, the system will seal them up for safekeeping automatically. In doing so, the questionnaires will only be seen by the respondents and researcher–avoiding any access to the third party—which also will avoid the internal misgivings of the respondents when they are submitting the questionnaires by hand. As a result, it will increase the privacy of the respondents, and enhance the authenticity of the respondent's response to a certain extent (He, 2016).

Second is to increase the integrity and availability of filling in the questionnaires. Wang (2014) during the process of eliminating the invalid questionnaires in his investigation discovered that although the researcher stressed the importance of the questionnaire integrity time and time again, there still were many invalid questionnaires because some respondents had missed the questions by mistake or on purpose, or they had made multiple choices for single-choice questions, hence the effective recovery rate of the questionnaires was reduced. The form of an online survey could effectively avoid the omissions or mistakes with the help of the computer system. The questionnaires cannot be submitted, and the online system will point out the specific operational errors for the respondents, when the respondents have omitted the questions or made multiple choices for the single-choice questions.

Thirdly, it is convenient, flexible and could improve efficiency (Couper, 2012). For the respondents, they could have more flexible time and more private environment to fill in the questionnaires by adopting the online questionnaires, which will be helpful to improve the quality and authenticity. For the researchers, it could reduce the research cost, save the time to issue and collect the questionnaires. In addition, it is also capable of collecting data of higher quality from a wide range within a short time to improve the research quality. As it has lowered the utilization of paper, the research is more environment-friendly (Couper, 2012). The most important is that the online questionnaires could import data into the analysis software like Excel or SPSS directly after being completed, which will not only reduce the workload of data import but also effectively guarantee the accuracy and efficiency of data collection.

Compared with the paper questionnaire, although the online questionnaire has many advantages, it also has some shortcomings. The biggest weakness is that the response rate of the online questionnaire is often low compared to the paper questionnaire (Nulty, 2008). In this study, the researcher conducted an online questionnaire survey with the help of the human resources departments of newly-established universities in Sichuan. The authority and deterrence of the human resources department in the university can help increase the response rate to the questionnaire.

3.5.2 Procedure of Data Collection

1. Uploading the questionnaires

At present, China has several powerful and large online platforms for questionnaire survey providing free and paid service, such as www.wenjuan.com, www.wjx.cn, https://wj.qq.com. The researcher selected the most suitable network platform to upload the questionnaires and designed the questionnaire page online to make it presentable, graceful and convenient for the participants to answer the questions online. In the meantime, the researcher set the open grade, access and password, etc.

2. Acquiring the introduction letter from the university where the researcher works

Obtaining the introduction letter can make the survey more official and can help the researcher get better cooperation from participants. Furthermore, from an ethical point of view, this is also necessary for research. The researcher ensured that the Email received by the participant contains the electronic scanning file of the introduction letter of the university where the researcher works. Therefore, the grassroots administrative staff in newly-established universities who are involved in this study can rest assured that their participation is legal, important and necessary due to the concern and attention of the university.

3. Contacting the human resource departments of newly-established universities

The human resource departments of universities are the most familiar with the situations and information of faculty in their own universities, including the grassroots administrative staff. During the researcher's 14 years of work experience in human resources management of the university, the researcher has built the working relationships with the human resource departments of most of the newly-established universities in Sichuan. In this study, the researcher visited the human resource departments of newly-established universities in person, briefly introduced the questionnaire survey to them and asked for their help.

4. Distributing questionnaires

The researchers published the questionnaire on the "Wen Juan Xing" website, one of the largest online survey sites in China. At the same time, the researcher sent the electronic scanning file of the introduction letter, the link address of the questionnaire, electronic-invitation letter and the login password of the questionnaire to the human resource departments in newly-established universities in Sichuan. After receiving the relevant materials on the internet, each human resources department invited the grassroots administrative staff of their respective universities to participate in the survey and fill in the online questionnaire.

5. Collecting and aggregating the questionnaires

The researcher can timely see how many network questionnaires have been finished, so that he can determine when to end the questionnaire survey according to the quantity of the effective questionnaires. The recovery rate of the effective questionnaires shall be counted at the same time of eliminating the invalid questionnaires from the recovered questionnaires. American sociologist, Earl Babbie (2000), proposed a simple hierarchical rule: It is quite poor for research if the effective recovery rate of the questionnaire is lower than 50%. It is basically adequate for research if the effective recovery rate is at least 50%. It is good for research if the effective recovery rate reaches 60%. It is perfect for research if the effective recovery rate is more than 70%.

In addition, He (2016) suggests the following principles to eliminate the invalid questionnaires: (1) The answers of all questions are the same. (2) There are missing values for the questions or personal information part. (3) The answers present the regular changes, i.e., circulating as 1, 2, 3, 4, 5.

The researcher ended the questionnaire survey and started the data analysis when the respondents of the questionnaire were more than 400.

3.6 Study Ethics

Study ethics is an important concern when people are involved as participants in research (Johnson, 2010). There are three objectives to study ethics. The first is to protect human participants. The second is to ensure that the survey is conducted in a way that serves the interests of individuals, groups or society. The third is to examine the ethical soundness of the specific activities and projects in research, such as risk management, confidential protection, and the process of informed consent (Johnson, 2010). Hence, study ethics is important in the study.

Since the study involved the collection of data from those participants who are engaged in administration in established universities in Sichuan, China, care was given in order to maintain the credibility of the participants as well as their privacy. Hence, participation in the survey was on a voluntary basis where all of the respondents were not forced to participate and the confidentiality of the data would be protected against any third parties. On the other hand, participants do not need to provide any direct personal identification in the investigation, such as their names, the number of the identity card or other private information, which may disclose their identities. In addition, introduction letter from the university where the researcher works can obtain prior to the survey so that grassroots administrative staff in newly-established universities can rest assured that their participation is legal, important and necessary due to the concern and attention of the university.

3.7 Data Analysis Techniques

In this study, Statistical Package for the Social Sciences (SPSS) and Amos are utilized to conduct the process of data analysis. To answer Research Question 1, the data screening, such as the patterns of missing data, identification of outliers, normality test, and analysis of respondents' profile are conducted by using SPSS. In order to answer Research Questions 2- 4, which seek to explore the relationship among variables and examine the hypotheses in line with research questions, a structural model is carried out by using AMOS. The data analysis techniques employed by the study are explained below:

3.7.1 Data Screening and Non-Response Bias

As an initial and important step in data analysis, data screening is conducted firstly to test the inconsistent and missing data, outliers among respondents, the normality of data, and common method variance. Therefore, whether the data set of the study are well-modeled by a normal distribution can be checked. Moreover, non-response bias and normality test are also conducted in the preliminary analysis.

3.7.2 Descriptive Statistical Analysis

Descriptive analysis can be described as the characteristics of the respondents. Meanwhile, in order to measure mean, mode, frequency, standard deviation and ranges, descriptive analysis was used to demonstrate the sample data by describing the representatives of respondents and showing the common types of responses (Burns and Bush, 2005). In this study, the descriptive statistical analysis consists mainly of two parts: One part is the descriptive statistics of the demographic samples which is used to analyze the relative frequency and percent frequency distributions of demographic variables, such as sex, marital status, education background. The other part is the descriptive statistics of observed variables, including perceived organizational support, work engagement, and job performance in order to obtain preliminary information on the mean and variance of each variable.

3.7.3 Multicollinearity/Correlation Matrix Test

Multicollinearity is a problem presented in regression analysis when there is a great or very high correlation among the exogenous (independent variables) (Sekaran, 2003). Hence, the predictive ability of the exogenous variables on the endogenous variable can be affected significantly by multicollinearity.

Multicollinearity test is used to check the degree of correlation matrix among exogenous variables. According to Cooper and Schindler (2014) and Creswell (2003, 2007, 2009), a correlation coefficient of 0.80 and above represents multicollinearity between independent variables. In addition, another statistical test is conducted to examine the presence of multicollinearity with the use of the tolerance, conditional index and variance inflated factors (VIF) according to the suggestion of Hair, Hult, Ringle and Sarstedt (2014).

3.7.4　Testing the Goodness of the Measurement Instrument

Two techniques are used to test the goodness of the instrument. One is the reliability test and the other one is factor analysis for assessing the validity of data.

1. Reliability test

Reliability refers to the extent to which the measurement is consistent and free from errors (Zikmund, 2003). Bolarinwa (2015) pointed out that the measurement of reliability is testing the consistency and stability of the instrument items or variables. The reliability test is done to improve the level of reliability of an instrument survey. The value of Cronbach's alpha is to measure and test the reliability of a questionnaire due to internal consistency.

The reliability coefficient should be between 0 and 1, and the higher the value of the alpha coefficient, the higher the reliability of the survey instrument used in the study. Precisely, if the alpha coefficient value of the scale is above 0.9, it means that the reliability of the scale is excellent; if the alpha coefficient value ranges from 0.8 to 0.9, it means the reliability is very good; if the alpha coefficient value of the scale is between 0.7 and 0.8, it means that the reliability is also good, but maybe some items of the scale need to be revised; if the reliability coefficient of the scale is below 0.7, it means that the reliability is not good and some items of the scale need to be discarded (Hair et al., 2006). Table 3.7 below shows the level of acceptability of the instrument.

Table 3.7 *The Level of Acceptability of the Instrument Proposed by Hair et al. (2006).*

Alpha Coefficient Range	Strength of Association
< 0.6	Poor
0.6 - 0.7	Moderate
0.7 - 0.8	Good
0.8 - 0.9	Very good
> 0.9	Excellent

Scales of questionnaire utilized in this study were already tested many times, and all were adopted from the published work and high attention and care were observed to warrant the reliability of collected data. Even so, Cronbach's Alpha is adopted in this study again to ensure the reliability of the survey.

2. Validity analysis

In order to examine the validity of the measurements statistically, factor analysis is carried out. Factor analysis can be defined as "a set of techniques for studying interrelationships among variables" (Weiers, 2011: 114). It is used to reduce data to a smaller set of summary variables and to explore the underlying theoretical structure of the phenomena. It is also useful to identify the structure of the relationship between the variable and the respondent (Henson and Roberts, 2006). Validity is the degree to which a measurement tool or means can accurately measure what is needed. In order to ensure the validity of the measurement instrument, this study used EFA to test the validity of the pilot study. Furthermore, EFA is also used to examine the validity of the final collected data.

3.7.5 Testing the Measurement Model

After testing the goodness of the measurement instrument by using SPSS, the data are analyzed through SEM by using AMOS software. SEM is a statistical technique used for testing the complex relationships among different variables (Hair et al., 2010). It can uses to examine the direct and indirect relationships for the proposed model. However, it is necessary to test the measurement model before examining the research hypotheses. Therefore, in this study, confirmatory factor analysis (CFA) is conducted to test several models, including CFA of perceived organizational support, CFA of work engagement and CFA of job performance. Besides that, discriminant validity and composite reliability are also tested in data analysis.

3.7.6 Structural Equation Modeling (SEM)

SEM is utilized for testing hypotheses because it is recommended to be adopted when the model is complex (Hair et al., 2006). There are three primary constructs, eight latent variables, fifty-six indicators, and a lot of hypotheses about their relationships in the study. Just using SPSS's multiple regression analysis may not be able to accurately and precisely figure the results. By utilizing SEM, the researcher can estimate the strength of the relationships and access how well the data actually fit the model with the relationship and path diagram specified (Hair et al., 2010). When multiple variables are used to indicate the constructs, SEM approach can also provide estimated values for exogenous constructs. According to Mackinnon, Lockwood and Hoffman (2002), SEM is flexible in incorporating multiple causes, mediators and moderators in on the single model. In this study, vigor, dedication and absorption are the mediators that are tested in the relationship between perceived organizational support and job performance. In this way, the hypotheses derived related to the research questions will all be tested.

3.8 Pilot Study

Because this study uses a questionnaire-based survey, the reliability and validity of the questionnaire must be confirmed prior to the actual survey. The significance of the pilot study has been stressed by Hair et al. (2006, 2010, 2014). It is imperative to conduct a pilot study so as to assist the researcher in building a great foundation for the major study. Validity means that the indicators used in the questionnaire represents the concept in an accurate manner, while reliability refers to the existence of the consistency between the indicators (Hair et al., 2006). Achieving reliability and validity of the questionnaire means that the questions asked are clear to the respondents, and the response options are appropriate and comprehensive (Watson, Clark and Tellegen, 1988). Such procedures can be achieved by conducting a pilot study which is strongly recommended to test the questionnaire (Hair et al., 2006; Watson et al., 1988).

In this study, the questionnaire was adopted from similar previous studies. Pre-Test of the questionnaire is required because the questionnaire is adopted from different geographical areas, from different research field, and the respondents are different. Such reasons require the researcher to do a pilot study to retest the questionnaire to identify its propriety of work in the Chinese university context. For the purpose of the pilot test, 82 questionnaires were distributed to grassroots administrative staff in 3 newly-established universities in Sichuan.

3.8.1 Reliability Test

Conducting the reliability test resulted in achieving Cronbach's alpha's values range from 0.936 to 0.947 more than the required 0.6 cuts of criterion that is generally regarded as sufficient for empirical research (Hair et al., 2006). Table 3.8 shows Cronbach's alpha's value for each variable.

Table 3.8 *Pilot Study Result for Reliability of the Questionnaire*

Variables	Dimensions	Numbers of items	Cronbach's Alpha
Perceived Organizational Support	Working Support	10	0.943
	Identifying Value	7	0.912
	Caring about Well-being	7	0.947

Continued

Variables	Dimensions	Numbers of items	Cronbach's Alpha
Work Engagement	Vigor	3	0.850
	Dedication	3	0.895
	Absorption	3	0.886
Job Performance	Task Performance	8	0.963
	Contextual Performance	15	0.974

From the table above, the results of the pilot study indicate that the Cronbach's Alpha for all variables is mostly above 0.9. Therefore, item elimination was not required. It can be concluded that the reliability coefficient of the pilot test was great and acceptable.

3.8.2 Validity Test

Validity test is required to determine the degree to which a measurement tool or instrument can accurately measure what needs to be measured. That is to say, the measured result reflects the degree of content that you want to examine (Neil et al., 2009). There are two ways of calibrating an instrument: the construct and content validity. Both construct and content validity are tested in this study.

For testing the construct validity of the questionnaire, EFA was conducted in the pilot study. This analysis technique can test the interrelationship among latent variables of the study and ensure the consistency of the extracted factors with their original and theoretical form (StataCorp, 2013).

The Bartlett Test of Sphericity (BTS) and the Kaise-Meyer-Olkin (KMO) measure of sampling are widely used for the correlations of the variables (Sekaran et al., 2016). The closer the KMO to 1.0, the smaller the sum of the partial correlation among all pairs of variables. The results of the pilot study indicate that the KMO ranged between 0.87 and 0.92 and Bartlett's test is extremely significant ($p = 0.000$), which means that the questionnaire is very suitable for factor analysis.

CHAPTER THREE : RESEARCH METHODOLOGY

In addition, according to Hair et al. (2010), the factor loadings of items in the instruments should be at least more than 0.50. Hair et al. (2014) further suggested that if the factor load of the problem exceeds 0.7, it would be better. Table 3.9 below shows that the factor loadings of all the items in the pilot study range from 0.58 to 0.89, and most of the factor loadings are above 0.7, which means that all the items can be retained and used in the final questionnaire survey.

Table 3.9 *Pilot Study Result for Factor Analysis of the Questionnaire*

Variables	Dimensions	Items	Loadings
Perceived Organizational Support	Working Support	WS9	0.841
		WS4	0.829
		WS1	0.816
		WS7	0.811
		WS6	0.799
		WS8	0.799
		WS10	0.786
		WS5	0.778
		WS3	0.756
		WS2	0.666
	Identifying Value	IV6	0.815
		IV2	0.807
		IV5	0.780
		IV7	0.776
		IV3	0.753
		IV1	0.745
		IV4	0.743

Continued

Variables	Dimensions	Items	Loadings
	Caring about Well-being	CW3	0.889
		CW6	0.865
		CW4	0.864
		CW5	0.863
		CW7	0.856
		CW2	0.819
		CW1	0.762
Work Engagement	Vigor	VI3	0.865
		VI2	0.695
		VI1	0.583
	Dedication	DE2	0.879
		DE1	0.814
		DE3	0.789
	Absorption	AB1	0.853
		AB3	0.832
		AB2	0.817
Job Performance	Task Performance	TP4	0.884
		TP8	0.857
		TP7	0.832
		TP1	0.827
		TP3	0.823
		TP2	0.809
		TP6	0.803
		TP5	0.769

Continued

Variables	Dimensions	Items	Loadings
	Contextual Performance	CP11	0.872
		CP12	0.837
		CP8	0.830
		CP13	0.828
		CP10	0.823
		CP3	0.789
		CP7	0.785
		CP5	0.785
		CP9	0.777
		CP6	0.770
		CP1	0.762
		CP4	0.758
		CP14	0.741
		CP15	0.719
		CP2	0.711

The content validity applied in the study was done by the submission of the instrument to the panel of experts and researchers within the field of management and education, so as to find whether the instrument for this study is within the linguistic capability of the respondents, and to ensure that the measurement measures what it is intended to measure (Sekaran and Bougie, 2009). It gives room for revision and adjustments. Thus, research instruments were subsequently improved.

Copies of the questionnaire were given to eight experts in newly-established universities in Sichuan, China, so as to obtain their suggestion and feedback on the content validity. Among them, one is the dean of the School of Education, one is the dean of the School of Management, two are the deputy directors of the Human Resources Management department, and the other five are professors of education or management. More basic information about them can be found in Appendix 2. From feedback, some of the experts thought that the content of the questionnaire and the statement of the items were appropriate and suitable, but some suggested that the expression of some items in the questionnaire should be corrected in order to make respondents understand them better. The adopted opinions of the experts are summarized in Table 3.10. However, the number of items in the three scales involved in the questionnaire was not increased or decreased, and the general meaning expressed in each item was not changed.

Table 3.10 *Expert's Main Suggestion for the Questionnaire*

Original items	Suggestion	Revised items
In majority of items of Perceived Organizational Support Scale (Chinese version), the subject of statements is the "单位"(work unit). For example, "The work unit can pay attention to my opinion at work"	The word "单位"(work unit) should be changed to "organization", so that it is more clear and consistent with the study	The word "单位"(work unit) was changed to "organization" in related items. For example, "The organization can pay attention to my opinion at work"
In several items of Job Performance Scale, the statement of the sentence has no subject. For example, "Volunteer for additional responsibilities"	The subject "I" should be added in the sentence to ensure that all items are expressed in the first person	The subject "I" was added in related items. For example, "I Volunteer for additional responsibilities"

Continued

Original items	Suggestion	Revised items
Item 4 in Work Engagement Scale: "I am active in my job"	"I am enthusiastic about my job" or "I am passionate about my job" are more suitable for context of work engagement	Item 4 in Work Engagement Scale was revised as "I am enthusiastic about my job"
Item 7 in Work Engagement Scale: "I am very happy when I am working intensely"	The word "very" must be removed, because words that express degree or frequency cannot exist in the sentence statement, which may affect the respondent's judgment	Item 7 in Work Engagement Scale was corrected as "I am happy when I am working intensely"
Item 1 in Job Performance Scale: "I always finish the work according to the standard operating procedures"	The word "always" must be removed, because words that reflect degree or frequency should not exist in the sentence statement, which may affect the respondent's judgment	Item 1 in Job Performance Scale was revised as "I finish the work according to the standard operating procedures"

3.9 Summary

Overall, this chapter explains about how the study is conducted. The quantitative research method is adopted in this study in order to explore the relationship between perceived organizational support, work engagement and job performance of grassroots administrative staff in newly-established universities. The target population is grassroots administrative staff in newly-established universities in Sichuan, China. The researcher employs Krejcie and Morgan's Table to estimate and determine the sampling size for this study. The research instrumentation in this study is a questionnaire made up of a series of questions to gather information from respondents, and it is adapted for this study and was carefully designed in content, structure and form. On the basis of literature review, intercomparison and consideration about Chinese cultural background, Ling et al.'s perceived organizational support scale, Schaufeli's Utrecht work engagement scale and Yu's job performance scale are used to form a questionnaire to measure the relevant variables of the study. The researcher uses an online survey to collect data. After data collection, SPSS and Amos are utilized to conduct the process of data analysis employing data screening, descriptive statistical analysis, reliability test, validity test, correlation analysis and SEM. Finally, the chapter discusses reliability and validity issues through the pilot study.

CHAPTER FOUR: DATA ANALYSIS AND RESULTS

4.1 Introduction

This chapter reports the data analysis and results. Firstly, the response rate, detection of missing data, detection of outliers, test of normality, test of common method variance, test of non-response bias, and descriptive analysis are conducted and discussed. Then, the chapter reports the reliability and factor analysis did to ensure the validity of the data used in the study.

It then goes on to provide information about how AMOS is used to conduct further data analysis and how confirmatory factor analysis is carried out to test the measurement model before examining the research hypotheses. It is followed by the discussion of Discriminant validity and composite. Then, the most crucial data analysis, that is, direct and indirect hypotheses test are reported, and the details of the testing results are presented. Finally, the research findings are concluded.

4.2 Response Rate

The population for this study is 3600 grassroots administrative staff of newly-established universities in Sichuan. Krejcie and Morgan (1970) suggested a sample of 351 for a population of 3500-4000, and Hinkle and Oliver (1983) suggested that a larger sampling size is more reliable. Therefore, based on this, the study was very cautious so as to prevent poor return rate that may fall below the minimum acceptable response. With the help of colleagues and friends, the researchers invited a total of 620 grassroots administrative staff from 9 universities to participate in the survey. The questionnaires are distributed by e-mail, QQ, WeChat, and the Office Automation (OA) system of the university.

Initially, many of the invitees were not interested in the survey, or held a skeptical or repulsive attitude. To overcome this obstacle, the researcher offered rewards to the survey participants to ensure the improvement of the response rate of the questionnaire. The entire survey began on 5th March, 2018 and ended on 13th July, 2018.

Of the 620 administrative staff invited to participate in the survey, a total of 426 responded and returned the questionnaires online, representing 68.71% of the sample size from this response rate. This was beyond expectations, because according to the literature, the response rate of the online questionnaire is often low compared to the paper questionnaire (Nulty, 2008).

There is no one exact answer about what an appropriate rate is (Morton, Bandara, Robinson and Carr, 2012), but response rates approximating 60% for most research should be the goal of researchers and expectation of the editors (Fincham, 2008). Moreover, it should also be pointed out that there is no missing data in the questionnaires, because the online survey system does not allow incomplete questionnaires to be submitted online.

Table 4.1 below shows the summary of the overall response rate for the study.

Table 4.1   *The Response Details*

Details	Rate
Number of distributed questionnaires	620
Returned questionnaires	426
Unusable questionnaires	0
Returned and usable questionnaires	426
Usable response rate	68.71%

CHAPTER FOUR : DATA ANALYSIS AND RESULTS

4.3 Data Preparation and Screening

Before conducting data analysis, it is essential to take into consideration the accuracy of the data entered into the data file, hence the results of data analysis will not be misled and wrong (Tabachinick, Fidell, and Ullman, 2007). This section discusses the necessary data screening procedures prior to data analysis which is the detection of missing data and outliers as these invalid values may threaten the validity of the study findings and must be identified and dealt with (Hair et al., 2010).

4.3.1 Detection of Missing Data

Missing data means that data value is not stored in a variable in the observation of interest (Hair et al., 2006). In other words, missing data occurs when the respondents did not answer one or more questions in the survey because of negligence, reluctance, or other reasons. According to Cohen, Cohen, West and Aiken (2013), some serious problems may be caused by the interpretation of the findings if missing data is up to 10% or more. Fortunately, an electronic questionnaire was used as a collection technique in the study, and the survey was conducted online. This data collection method can effectively prevent the generation of missing data and ensure that all items are answered fully by respondents, by having the system automatically block incomplete e-questionnaires from being submitted. Therefore, missing data was not an issue in this research.

4.3.2 Detection of Outliers

It is quite necessary to detect any influential outliers before conducting data analysis. In the study, Mahalanobis distance (d^2) was utilized to assess outliers. Based on 61 observed variables in the study, the recommended chi-square critical value is 100.89 at $p=0.001$. Mahalanobis values that were exceeded this threshold should be deleted. Therefore, twenty-eight cases of multivariate outliers were determined and subsequently deleted from the data collection. The remaining 398 respondents were used for the final data analysis and hypothesis tests.

Table 4.2 *The Outliers of the Study Based on Mahalanobis Distance Value*

Number	Observation cases	Mahalanobis d^2
1	229	143.68952
2	58	136.19117
3	196	129.38155
4	351	123.67357
5	172	122.14980
6	224	119.38804
7	27	113.55707
8	403	113.12911
9	176	112.79808
10	163	112.49286
11	310	110.26555
12	20	110.13109
13	139	108.89376
14	141	106.57414
15	263	105.85313
16	136	105.06930
17	408	104.73791
18	121	103.30769
19	133	102.76799
20	234	102.74389
21	126	102.41288
22	293	102.24861

Continued

Number	Observation cases	Mahalanobis d²
23	369	102.11250
24	22	101.67967
25	355	101.57907
26	397	101.49580
27	46	101.40346
28	391	101.38823

4.3.3 Test of Normality

According to Hair et al. (2010), normality is regarded as the imperative assumption in multivariate analysis. This is because unreliable results may be led by any substantial violation of this assumption. Generally, normality means that the data distribute symmetrically, and this kind of distribution forms the greatest frequency around the mean that shapes the bell curve (Pallant, 2005).

There are several different ways to test normality, such as the use of visual tools (e.g., stem and leaf plots, normal P-P plot), Kolmogorov-Smirnov tests (Mooi and Sarstedt, 2011), and skewness and kurtosis (Hair et al., 2010). If there is a lack of normality in variable distribution, the relationship among the variables of the research may be distorted, and the results of the multivariate analysis may be distorted as well. In this study, the test for normality of data was conducted through not only the visual distribution, but also the statistical distribution of the data.

According to the suggestion by Tabachinick and Fidell (2007), if the number of samples exceeds 200, then observing the graphic distribution shape is more important than considering the Skewness and Kurtosis statistical test. Therefore, there are two steps for assessing normality in this study: the first step is to utilize the graphical method of normality, and the second step is to assess the values of Skewness and Kurtosis.

For the first step, a histogram and normal probability plots were used. The results showed in Figures 4.1 and 4.2 indicate that the collected data for the present study is quite normal.

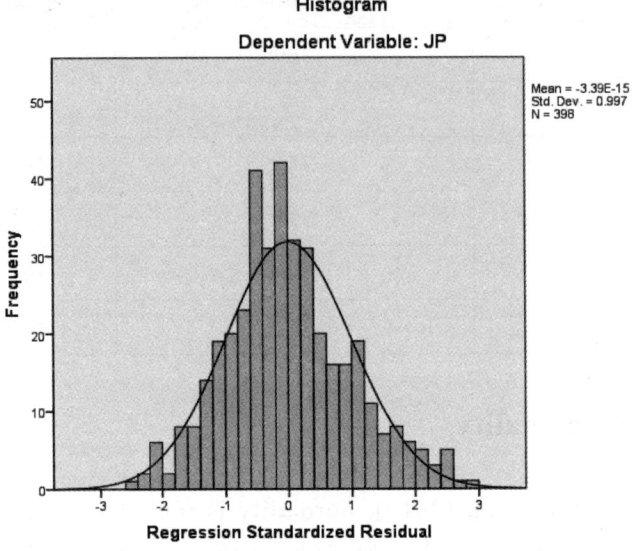

Figure 4.1. Histogram of Dependent Variable: Job Performance (JP)

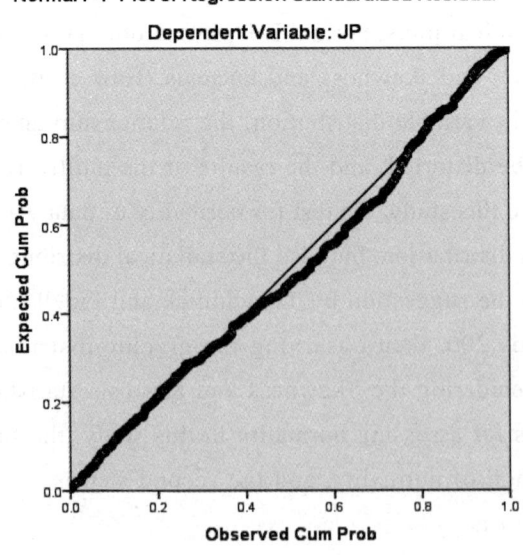

Figure 4.2. Normal P–P Plot of Regression Standardized Residual

For the second step, this study used skewness and kurtosis values which are recommended by many researchers to show the data distribution (Pallant, 2005).

Skewness is the extent to which the distribution of a variable is symmetrical while kurtosis measures the peak of the distribution. As a general rule, the values of skewness should be ranged between +1 and -1 for the data to be described as normal data (Hair et al., 2010). However, kurtosis values between -2 to +2 is still acceptable (George and Mallery, 2010), and according to the suggestion of Kline (1998), the threshold between +3 and -3 is also acceptable.

Table 4.3 below shows that the skewness values of all variables are within the range of +2 and -2. In fact, except for a value of 1.103, the skewness values of all others are between +1 and -1. Therefore, the data of this study can be considered to be in a normal distribution. In terms of kurtosis value which is an indicator to detect whether the data set are peaked or flat relative to a normal distribution, normally it is considered to range from +1 to -1 (Hair et al., 2010). However, kurtosis values between +2 and -2 are in many cases acceptable just like skewness (George and Mallery, 2010). In this study, all kurtosis values are within the range of +1 and -1.

Therefore, the test of skewness and kurtosis prove that the entire constructs and data are normal.

Table 4.3 *Values of Skewness and Kurtosis of Measured Variables*

Constructs	Dimensions	Skewness	Kurtosis
Perceived Organizational Support	Working Support	0.295	0.429
	Identifying Value	0.413	0.456
	Caring about Well-being	0.247	0.100
Work Engagement	Vigor	0.406	-0.74
	Dedication	0.159	0.053
	Absorption	0.017	-0.259
Job Performance	Task Performance	1.103	-0.174
	Contextual Performance	0.840	-0.318

4.3.4 Test of Common Method Variance

The common method bias refers to the artificial covariation between the predictor and the criterion variable caused by the same data source or scorer, the same measurement environment, the project context, and the characteristics of the project itself. This kind of artificial covariation is seriously confused with the research results and is potentially misleading (Lindell and Whitney, 2001). It is a systematic error. Common method biases are widespread in psychology, behavioral science research, and especially in the use of questionnaires. Therefore, it is necessary to detect the common method bias before verifying the hypothesis to avoid the existence of a common method bias misleading the research results. Three tests were carried out in the study to examine the common method bias.

The first test is using EFA. All 56 items were entered and the result of the analysis yielded eight factors explaining a cumulative of 76.02% of the variance, with the first (largest) factor explains 20.71% of the total variance which is lower than 50%. According to Podsakoff, MacKenzie and Podsakoff (2012), there is a lack of substantial common method bias.

Secondly, a confirmatory factor analysis (CFA) was conducted, and all 56 items were modeled as the indicators of a just single factor. However, the results indicate a poor fit , and it means that the common method bias is not a significant problem (Malhotra, Hall, Shaw, and Oppenheim, 2006).

Thirdly, the correlation matrix test also can be used to determine common method bias based on a suggestion by Bagozzi, Yi, and Phillips (1991). Namely, inter-construct correlations are all below 0.90 which mean there was no common method bias. The results shown in Table 4.11 indicate that common method bias is not a problem in the study.

4.4 Testing Non-response Bias

Non-response bias is an issue of a major concern when the researcher deals with survey methodology (Armstrong and Overton, 1977). Non-response bias is a bias caused by the research respondents' different responses to the research content. (Dillman, 2000). The validity of the survey can be threatened by non-response bias. If a non-responder is unwilling to answer any questions for some reason, or if a non-responder has a common characteristic, there may be a serious bias in the results of the study of respondents. (Lahaut, Jansen, Van de Mheen, and Garretsen, 2002).

Moreover, Malhotra, Hall, Shaw and Oppenheim (2006) argued that late respondents could be considered non-respondents because they would not respond if they were not repeatedly visited and reminded by researchers. It was compulsory to carry out non-response bias testing in this study for two reasons. Firstly, some of the respondents responded to the questionnaire after several reminders. Secondly, the whole data collection was carried out over a period of four months extending from March 2018 to July 2018.

In the study, T-test was conducted to assess non-response bias between early and late respondents. According to the suggestion of Armstrong and Overton (1977), there would be underlying differences between respondents and non-respondents if differences between late and early respondent are found to be significant.

The T-test was conducted between the 298 early and the 100 late respondents. All the variables including dimensions were taken into account.

Table 4.4 *Result of Non-Response Bias Test*

Constructs	Dimensions	Responses	N	Mean	P
Perceived Organizational Support	Working Support	Early Responses	298	2.7221	0.573
		Late Responses	100	2.7780	0.595
	Identifying Value	Early Responses	298	2.7680	0.959
		Late Responses	100	2.7629	0.958
	Caring about Well-being	Early Responses	298	2.8581	0.912
		Late Responses	100	2.8471	0.910
Work Engagement	Vigor	Early Responses	298	2.6857	0.522
		Late Responses	100	2.7467	0.529
	Dedication	Early Responses	298	2.6007	0.353
		Late Responses	100	2.6967	0.381
	Absorption	Early Responses	298	2.7494	0.601
		Late Responses	100	2.8033	0.613
Job Performance	Task Performance	Early Responses	298	2.5076	0.775
		Late Responses	100	2.4700	0.770
	Contextual Performance	Early Responses	298	2.5114	0.343
		Late Responses	100	2.6340	0.381

CHAPTER FOUR : DATA ANALYSIS AND RESULTS

4.5 Descriptive Analysis

4.5.1 Demographic Profile of the Respondents

The profile of the respondents was analyzed in the study by the researcher using their demographic characteristics in terms of gender, age, marital status, education level and academic rank. The more detailed analyses are presented as follows:

1. Respondents profile by gender

Out of the 398 valid responses used in the study, 187 (47.0%) of them are males while 211 (53.0%) are females. The number of respondents by gender is a reflection of the total number of male and female administrative staff in the universities.

Table 4.5 *Respondents Distribution by Gender*

Gender	Frequency	Percent
Male	187	47.0
Female	211	53.0
Total	426	100.0

2. Respondents profile by age

As revealed in the descriptive analysis of the respondents' age, the age group with the largest number of respondents is under 30 years old, with a total of 185 (46.5%). The second largest age group is 3039-year-old respondents, a total of 131, accounting for 32.9% of the total number of respondents. The respondents between the ages of 40 and 49 are 58 (14.6%), while the respondents aged 50 and above are the least, only 24 (6.0%). This shows that the employees of the newly-established university who are engaged in grassroots administrative work are relatively young. People under the age of 40 are the main body of university grassroots administrative workers, accounting for nearly 80% of the proportion.

Table 4.6   *Respondents Distribution by Age*

Age	Frequency	Percent
29 Years and below	185	46.5
30-39 Years	131	32.9
40-49 Years	58	14.6
50 Years and above	24	6.0
Total	398	100.0

3. Respondents profile by marital status

As revealed by the 398 valid responses, those who were not married accounted for 45.0% of the total number, with 179 people. More respondents were married, which is 219 and accounting for 55.0%.

Table 4.7   *Respondents Distribution by Marital Status*

Marital Status	Frequency	Percent
Unmarried	179	45.0
Married	219	55.0
Total	398	100.0

4. Respondents profile by education level

As saw in Table 4.8, 31 (7.8%) of the respondents are Ph.D holders, 146 (36.7%) are Master's degree holders. 207 (52.0%) have a Bachelor's degree while the remaining 14 respondents representing 3.5% of the total number of the valid questionnaire do not have a Bachelor's degree. This shows that the overall educational level of the grassroots administrative staff in newly-established universities is not high enough.

Table 4.8 *Respondents Distribution by Qualification*

Qualification	Frequency	Percent
Ph.D	31	7.8
Master	146	36.7
Bachelor	207	52.0
Diploma	14	3.5
Total	398	100.0

Note: The higher education system in China includes Doctoral, Master's, and Bachelor's degrees, as well as non-degree programs. Diploma refers to someone who has a university/college diploma but does not have a Bachelor's degree.

5. Respondents profile by academic rank

As showed in Table 4.9 below, the numbers of professors and associate professors are only 5 (1.2%) and 62 (15.6%) respectively, while 131 respondents representing 32.9% are lecturers. The remaining 200 people are assistants or have no academic rank. Overall, this indicates that the academic level of the grassroots administrative staff of the newly-established university is not high. Obviously, this phenomenon is related to the reform of university management system in China in recent years. For example, some universities in Sichuan no longer allow administrative staff to compete for academic rank as before. It should be said that the majority of administrative staff of the university have no energy or ability to carry out academic work with spare time, and some universities do not allow administrative staff to apply for academic ranks and titles. Therefore, the overall level of administrative staff's academic rank may continue to decrease.

Table 4.9 *Respondents Distribution by Academic Rank*

Academic Rank	Frequency	Percent
Professor	5	1.2
Associate Professor	62	15.6
Lecturer	131	32.9

Continued

Academic Rank	Frequency	Percent
Assistant lecturer or none	200	50.3
Total	398	100.0

Note: The academic rank system of higher education system in China includes four levels: professor, associate professor, lecturer, and assistant lecturer. Assistant lecturer or none refers to people who work as assistant lecturers or who do not have any academic ranks. They are at the lowest level of the academic rank system.

4.5.2 Descriptive Statistics of the Research Variables

The descriptive statistics for all variables in the study were computed by means and standard deviation. Five-point Likert scale from "totally disagree" ranked as point 1 at one end and "totally agree" ranked as point 5 on the other end, was adopted to measure the indicators for all the variables and dimensions of the study.

As can be seen from Table 4.10 below the mean values of the three constructs are all below 3 points, of which the perceived organizational support is a little higher at 2.78, while the job performance is the lowest, accounting for only 2.53. This shows the perceived organizational support, work engagement, and job performance among grassroots administrative staff in newly-established universities of Sichuan, China is just at a slightly lower level. Next, the table shows more latent variables, which are the dimensions of the three constructs. In terms of perceived organizational support, caring about well-being (2.86) is the highest while working support (2.74) is the lowest. That is to say, the administrative staff thinks that the university's support for their work is not enough. In terms of work engagement, absorption (2.76) is the highest and dedication (2.62) is the lowest, whereas in terms of job performance, the mean values of task performance (2.50) and contextual performance (2.54) are almost the same, both at a relatively low level.

CHAPTER FOUR : DATA ANALYSIS AND RESULTS

Table 4.10 *Descriptive Statistics for all Variables of the Study*

Constructs	Dimensions	N	Mean	Std. Deviation
Perceived Organizational Support		398	2.7798	0.69311
	Working Support	398	2.7362	0.85615
	Identifying Value	398	2.7667	0.86936
	Caring about Well-being	398	2.8553	0.85777
Work Engagement		398	2.6963	0.72395
	Vigor	398	2.7010	0.82380
	Dedication	398	2.6248	0.89244
	Absorption	398	2.7630	0.89119
Job Performance		398	2.5269	1.04223
	Task Performance	398	2.4981	1.13303
	Contextual Performance	398	2.5422	1.11679

4.6 Multicollinearity/Correlation Matrix Test

Multicollinearity is a problem that occurs with regression analysis when there is a great or very high correlation among the exogenous (independent variables). Hence, the predictive ability of the exogenous variables on the endogenous variable can be affected significantly by multicollinearity.

Multicollinearity test is means to check the degree of the correlation matrix among exogenous variables. According to Cooper and Schindler (2014) and Sekaran (2003), a correlation coefficient of 0.80 and above represents multicollinearity between independent variables. However, other researchers Hair et al. (2010) suggested that the correlation coefficient should be no problem if it does not exceed a value of 0.90. As the results are shown in Table 4.11, all the variables are positively correlated, but there is no multicollinearity among all the exogenous latent variables (working support, identifying value, caring about well-being, vigor, dedication, absorption) since all the correlation coefficients are lower than 0.8 and significant at the 0.01 level (2-tailed).

Table 4.11 *Correlation Matrix is among the Exogenous Latent Variables*

Exogenous Variables	1	2	3	4	5	6
Working Support	1					
Identifying Value	0.512**	1				
Caring about Well-being	0.434**	0.443**	1			
Vigor	0.453**	0.391**	0.428**	1		
Dedication	0.454**	0.471**	0.399**	0.541**	1	
Absorption	0.496**	0.428**	0.440**	0.485**	0.591**	1

**Significant at a level of 0.01

In addition, a statistical test was conducted to examine the presence of multicollinearity with the use of the tolerance, conditional index and variance inflated factors (VIF) according to the suggestion of Hair et al., (2014). This method is also considered reliable in testing multicollinearity. Hair et al. (2014) argued that multicollinearity exists when the tolerance value is less than 0.20, or VIF value is more than 5, or a conditional index is higher than 30. However, the results presented in Table 4.12 below reveal that all the observed values, including tolerance, VIF, conditional index are within a fully acceptable range, which indicates again, there is no problem for multicollinearity in the study.

Table 4.12 *Collinearity Statistics*

Exogenous Variables	Tolerance	VIF	Conditional Index
Working Support	0.601	1.665	10.089
Identifying Value	0.629	1.589	11.154
Caring about Well-being	0.679	1.473	12.074
Vigor	0.613	1.632	12.091
Dedication	0.531	1.884	12.856
Absorption	0.551	1.815	13.898

4.7 Testing the Goodness of the Measurement Instrument

Two techniques are used to test the goodness of the measurement instrument. One is the reliability test and the other one is factor analysis for assessing the validity of data.

4.7.1 Reliability Test

Reliability refers to the degree to which the results obtained are consistent when the same method is repeated for the same object (Hair et al., 2010). In other words, reliability refers to the degree of reliability of the measured data. It measures through Cronbach's Alpha coefficients. As suggested by Hair et al. (2010), reliability is acceptable when α is between 0.70 and 0.80, reliability is good when α is between 0.80 and 0.90, reliability is excellent when α is higher than 0.90. Table 4.13 shows the detailed result for reliability test, where all values range from 0.842 to 0.977 which are all higher than 0.80 value. Hence, all the variables included in the study show a quite good level of internal consistency.

Table 4.13 *Result for Reliability Test*

Variables	Dimensions	Number of Items	Cronbach's Alpha
Perceived Organizational Support	Working Support	10	0.957
	Identifying Value	7	0.930
	Caring about Well-being	7	0.936
Work Engagement	Vigor	3	0.852
	Dedication	3	0.860
	Absorption	3	0.842
Job Performance	Task Performance	8	0.976
	Contextual Performance	15	0.977

4.7.2 Exploratory Factor Analysis (EFA)

Validity refers to the extent to which a survey instrument can accurately measure what is needs for measurement. A survey instrument is considered valid when the measured result reflects the degree of content that you want to examine. The more consistent the measurement result is the content to be examined, the higher the validity; otherwise, the lower the validity (Hair et al., 2010).

This study used EFA to test the validity, although it has been tested in the previous pilot study.

As presented in Table 4.14, KMO values of all constructs, including their dimensions ranged between 0.87 and 0.97, meaning that KMO values are all higher than 0.50. Meanwhile, Bartlett's test of sphericity is significant with $p<0.05$. Thereby, the appropriateness of factor analysis is approved according to the suggestion by Hair et al. (2010).

CHAPTER FOUR: DATA ANALYSIS AND RESULTS

Table 4.14 *Factor Analysis Results*

Variables	Number of Items	KMO	Bartlett's Test of Sphericity Sig.
Perceived Organizational Support	24	0.962	0.000
Work Engagement	9	0.866	0.000
Job Performance	23	0.969	0.000

1. EFA of Perceived Organizational Support

The three dimensions of perceived organizational support including working support, identifying value and caring about well-being were measured for 24 items. The factor loadings of these items were measured using a rotated component matrix. According to Hair et al. (2010), the minimum benchmark of factor loadings is 0.50.

From Table 4.15, it can be seen that all 24 items are loading on three components with factor loadings values all higher than 0.7. Furthermore, the cumulative variance explained (CVE) indicates that these three components explained 71.97% of the overall variance in the construct of perceived organizational support. Eigenvalues of three components are greater than 1.0 as it is shown in the scree plot in Figure 4.3.

Table 4.15 *EFA for Construct of Perceived Organizational Support*

Items	Component		
	1	2	3
Working Support 6	.845		
Working Support 7	.833		
Working Support 9	.833		
Working Support 4	.816		
Working Support 5	.808		

Continued

Items	Component		
	1	2	3
Working Support 8	.808		
Working Support 1	.804		
Working Support 10	.804		
Working Support 2	.799		
Working Support 3	.735		
Caring about Well-being 4		.842	
Caring about Well-being 7		.836	
Caring about Well-being 5		.825	
Caring about Well-being 6		.820	
Caring about Well-being 2		.816	
Caring about Well-being 3		.807	
Caring about Well-being 1		.749	
Identifying Value 2			.822
Identifying Value 1			.810
Identifying Value 5			.804
Identifying Value 7			.794
Identifying Value 6			.786
Identifying Value 4			.770
Identifying Value 3			.757
Eigen Value	11.263	3.330	2.684
% of Variance	46.930	13.874	11.170
% of Total Variance Explained			71.974

CHAPTER FOUR : DATA ANALYSIS AND RESULTS

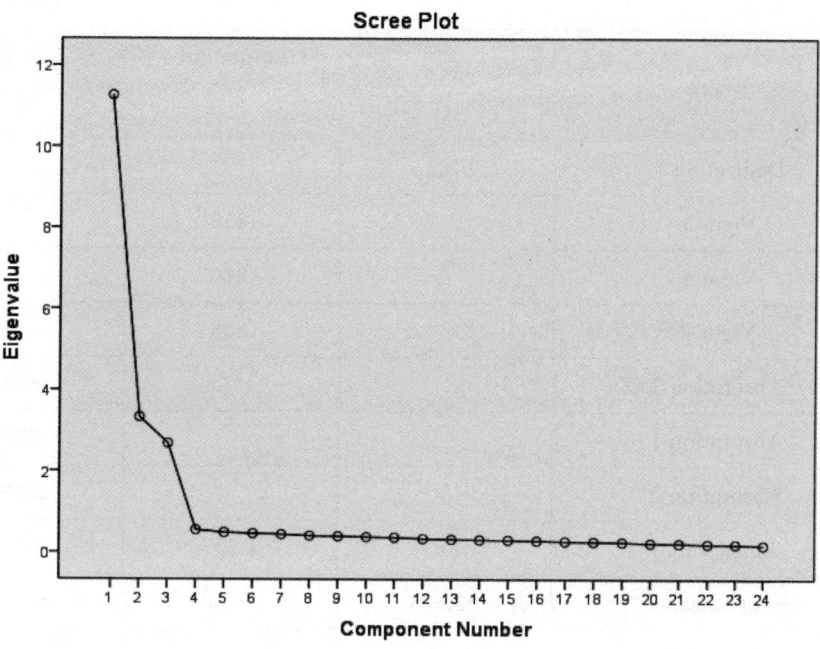

Figure 4.3. Scree Plot of Perceived Organizational Support

2. EFA of Work Engagement

Nine items are representing work engagement construct were sent to the factor analysis to identify the underlying factors. Table 4.16 reveals that, as expected, all nine items are loaded on three factors with factor loadings from 0.75 to 0.89, and the CVE explained 77.97% of the variance in the work engagement. In addition, the Eigenvalues of the three components are greater than 1.0 as it is shown in the scree plot in Figure 4.4.

Table 4.16 *EFA for Construct of Work Engagement*

Items	Component		
	1	2	3
Dedication 2	.838		
Dedication 3	.821		

Continued

Items	Component		
	1	2	3
Dedication 1	.782		
Vigor 3		.856	
Vigor 1		.816	
Vigor 2		.808	
Absorption 3			.890
Absorption 1			.787
Absorption 2			.749
Eigen Value	4.83	1.237	1.049
% of Variance	53.683	13.740	10.548
% of Total Variance Explained			77.971

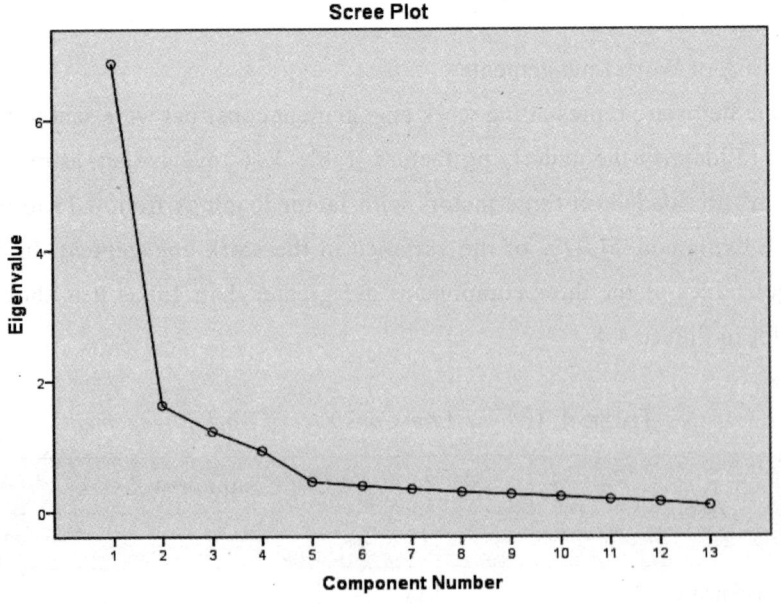

Figure 4.4. Scree Plot of Work Engagement

CHAPTER FOUR : DATA ANALYSIS AND RESULTS

3. EFA of Job Performance

Similarly, EFA was carried out to identify the dimensions underlying the construct of job performance. Table 4.17 shows that factor loading of 23 items ranges between 0.70 and 0.87, and all items are loaded on two components, and these two factors explained a total of 79.5% of the overall variance in the job performance. Also, the Eigenvalues of the two components are all greater than 1.0 as presented in Figure 4.5.

Table 4.17 *EFA for Construct of Job Performance*

Items	Component	
	1	2
Contextual Performance 11	.860	
Contextual Performance 12	.860	
Contextual Performance 13	.845	
Contextual Performance 8	.836	
Contextual Performance 9	.827	
Contextual Performance 10	.825	
Contextual Performance 6	.815	
Contextual Performance 14	.809	
Contextual Performance 4	.799	
Contextual Performance 5	.796	
Contextual Performance 7	.792	
Contextual Performance 2	.777	
Contextual Performance 3	.757	
Contextual Performance 1	.753	
Contextual Performance 15	.699	
Task Performance 3		.874
Task Performance 6		.866

Continued

Items	Component	
	1	2
Task Performance 4		.866
Task Performance 5		.864
Task Performance 2		.864
Task Performance 1		.852
Task Performance 8		.851
Task Performance 7		.836
Eigen Value	15.683	2.602
% of Variance	68.187	11.313
% of Total Variance Explained		79.500

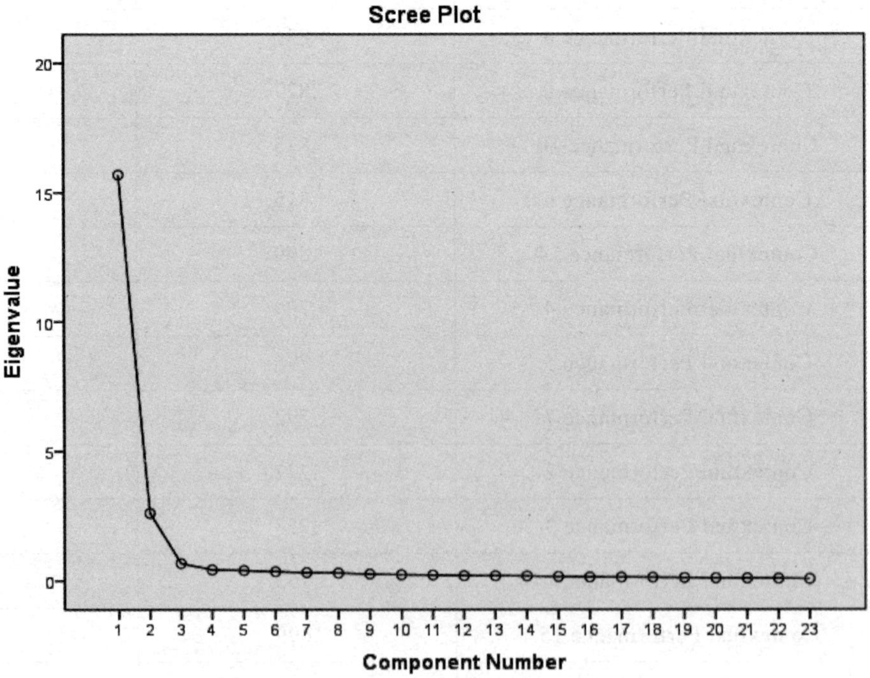

Figure 4.5. Scree Plot of Job Performance

4.7.3 Testing the Measurement Model

After testing the goodness of the measurement instrument by using SPSS, the data was analyzed through SEM by using AMOS software. SEM is a statistical technique used for testing the complex relationships among different variables (Hair et al., 2010). It can be used to examine the direct and indirect relationships for the proposed model. However, it is necessary to test the measurement model before examining the research hypotheses.

4.7.3.1 Confirmatory Factor Analysis (CFA)

1. CFA of perceived organizational support

Table 4.18 shows that the factor loadings on the items of perceiving organizational support is satisfactory, ranging from 0.71 to 0.87; this is considered acceptable as suggested by Hair et al. (2006). Therefore, it can concludes that all constructs meet the construct validity criterion. The number of items for each variable is as follows: working support (10 items), identifying value (7 items), caring about well-being (7 items).

Table 4.18 *Factor Loading of Construct of Perceived Organizational Support*

Variables	Items	Loadings
Working Support	WS1	0.837
	WS2	0.820
	WS3	0.712
	WS4	0.856
	WS5	0.831
	WS6	0.872
	WS7	0.865
	WS8	0.838
	WS9	0.855

Continued

Variables	Items	Loadings
	WS10	0.829
Identifying Value	IV1	0.832
	IV2	0.833
	IV3	0.765
	IV4	0.780
	IV5	0.822
	IV6	0.819
	IV7	0.825
Caring about Well-being	CW1	0.735
	CW2	0.833
	CW3	0.813
	CW4	0.840
	CW5	0.846
	CW6	0.849
	CW7	0.842

In addition, several indices were adopted to identify the goodness of fit of the exogenous model. For instance, the model of factors of the perceived organizational support as showed in Figure 4.6 yielded an expected significant chi-square (324.915, p=0.001) given the large sample size employed in the study. Other fit indices as shown in Table 4.19 also can be used to support chi-square and ensure the goodness of fit (e.g., Ratio=1.305, GFI=0.937, NFI=0.960, TLI=0.989, CFI=0.990, and RMSEA=0.028). From these indices, it can be seen that the model has achieved excellent fit for the data (Hair et al., 2010).

Table 4.19 *Good-Fit-Indices of Construct of Perceived Organizational Support*

Measures	Fit indices	Threshold Values	Source
Ratio	1.305	≤5	Marsh and Hocevar (1985); Schumacker and Lomax (2004)
GFI	0.937	≥0.8	Greenspoon and Saklofske (1998); Hair et al. (2010)
NFI	0.960	≥0.8	Greenspoon and Saklofske (1998); Forza and Filippini (1998)
CFI	0.990	≥0.9	Bentler (1990); Hair et al. (2010)
TLI	0.989	≥0.9	Hair et al. (2010); Awang (2012)
RMSEA	0.028	≤0.08	Greenspoon and Saklofske (1998); Byrne (2001); Awang (2012)

More details are shown in Figure 4.6.

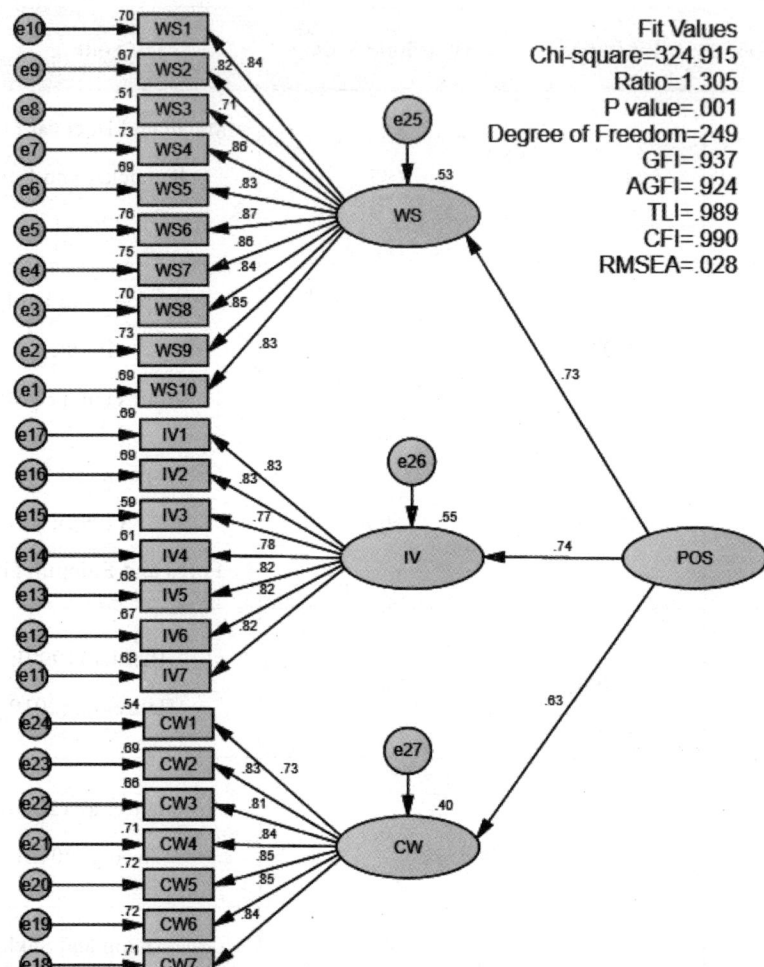

Figure 4.6. CFA for Construct of Perceived Organizational Support

2. CFA of Work Engagement

Confirmatory factor analysis was conducted on the construction of work engagement, which is the mediator. The results in Table 4.20 and Figure 4.7 indicate that factor loading of all items of relationship quality dimensions is satisfactory. Therefore, it can concludes that all constructs meet the construct validity criterion. The number of items for each variable is as follows: vigor (3 items), dedication (3 items), absorption (3 items).

Table 4.20 *Factor Loading of Construct of Work Engagement*

Variables	Items	Loadings
Vigor	VI3	.744
	VI2	.894
	VI1	.790
Dedication	DE3	.807
	DE2	.865
	DE1	.801
Absorption	AB3	.818
	AB2	.760
	AB1	.825

Furthermore, several indices were adopted to identify the goodness of fit of the model. For instance, the model of factors of the work engagement as shown in Table 4.21 and Figure 4.7 yielded an expected significant chi-square (87.712, p=0.000) given the large sample size employed in the study.

Other fit indices as showed in Table 4.21 also can be used to support chi-square and ensure the goodness of fit (e.g., Ratio=3.655, GFI=0.955, NFI=0.956, TLI=0.952, CFI=0.968, and RMSEA=0.079).

From these indices, it can be seen that the model has achieved good fit for the data (Hair et al., 2010).

Table 4.21 *Good-Fit-Indices of Construct of Work Engagement*

Measures	Fit indices	Threshold Values	Source
Ratio	3.655	≤5	Marsh and Hocevar (1985); Schumacker and Lomax (2004)
GFI	0.955	≥0.8	Greenspoon and Saklofske (1998); Hair et al. (2010)
NFI	0.956	≥0.8	Greenspoon and Saklofske (1998); Forza and Filippini (1998)
CFI	0.968	≥0.9	Bentler (1990); Hair et al. (2010)
TLI	0.952	≥0.9	Hair et al. (2010); Awang (2012)
RMSEA	0.079	≤0.08	Greenspoon and Saklofske (1998); Byrne (2001); Awang (2012)

More details about CFA for the construction of work engagement are shown in Figure 4.7 below.

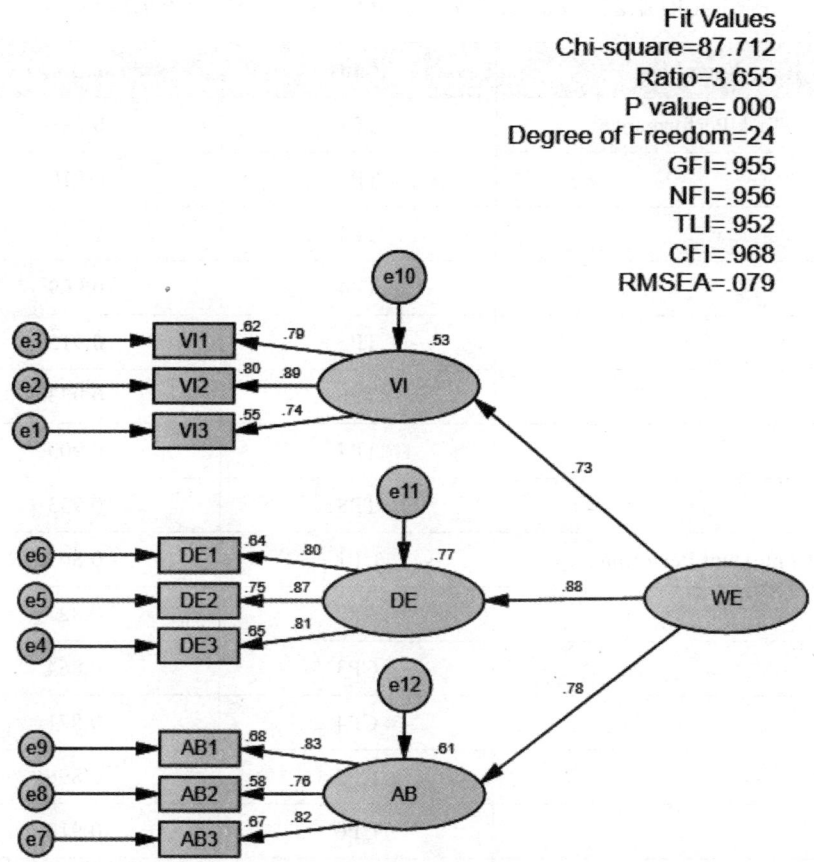

Figure 4.7. CFA for Construct of Perceived Organizational Support

3. CFA of Job Performance

Confirmatory factor analysis was conducted on the construction of job performance, which is the dependent variable. The results in Table 4.22 and Figure 4.8 indicate the factor loading of all items of relationship quality dimensions are satisfactory, ranging from 0.71 to 0.93, which exceeded the recommended value by Hair et al. (2006). Therefore, it can says that all constructs meet the construct validity criterion. The number of items for each variable is as follows: task

145

performance (8 items), contextual performance (15 items).

Table 4.22　*Factor Loading of Construct of Job Performance*

Variables	Items	Loadings
Task Performance	TP1	0.881
	TP2	0.910
	TP3	0.899
	TP4	0.909
	TP5	0.915
	TP6	0.923
	TP7	0.909
	TP8	0.933
Contextual Performance	CP1	0.805
	CP2	0.827
	CP3	0.864
	CP4	0.871
	CP5	0.896
	CP6	0.913
	CP7	0.875
	CP8	0.914
	CP9	0.909
	CP10	0.846
	CP11	0.896
	CP12	0.897
	CP13	0.879
	CP14	0.773
	CP15	0.708

Furthermore, several indices were adopted to identify the goodness of fit of the model. For instance, the modified model of factors of the work engagement as showed in Table 4.23 and Figure 4.8 yielded an expected significant chi-square (737.133, p=0.000) given the large sample size employed in the study. Other fit indices as shown in Table 4.23 also can be used to support chi-square and ensure the goodness of fit (e.g., Ratio=3.178, GFI=0.863, NFI=0.943, TLI=0.955, CFI=0.960, and RMSEA=0.074). From these indices, it can be seen that the model has achieved good fit for the data (Hair et al., 2010).

Table 4.23 *Good-Fit-Indices of Construct of Work Engagement*

Measures	Fit indices	Threshold Values	Source
Ratio	3.178	≤5	Marsh and Hocevar (1985); Schumacker and Lomax (2004)
GFI	0.863	≥0.8	Greenspoon and Saklofske (1998); Hair et al. (2010)
NFI	0.943	≥0.8	Greenspoon and Saklofske (1998); Forza and Filippini (1998)
CFI	0.960	≥0.9	Bentler (1990); Hair et al. (2010)
TLI	0.955	≥0.9	Hair et al. (2010); Awang (2012)
RMSEA	0.074	≤0.08	Greenspoon and Saklofske (1998); Byrne (2001); Awang (2012)

More details about CFA for work engagement are shown in Figure 4.8 below.

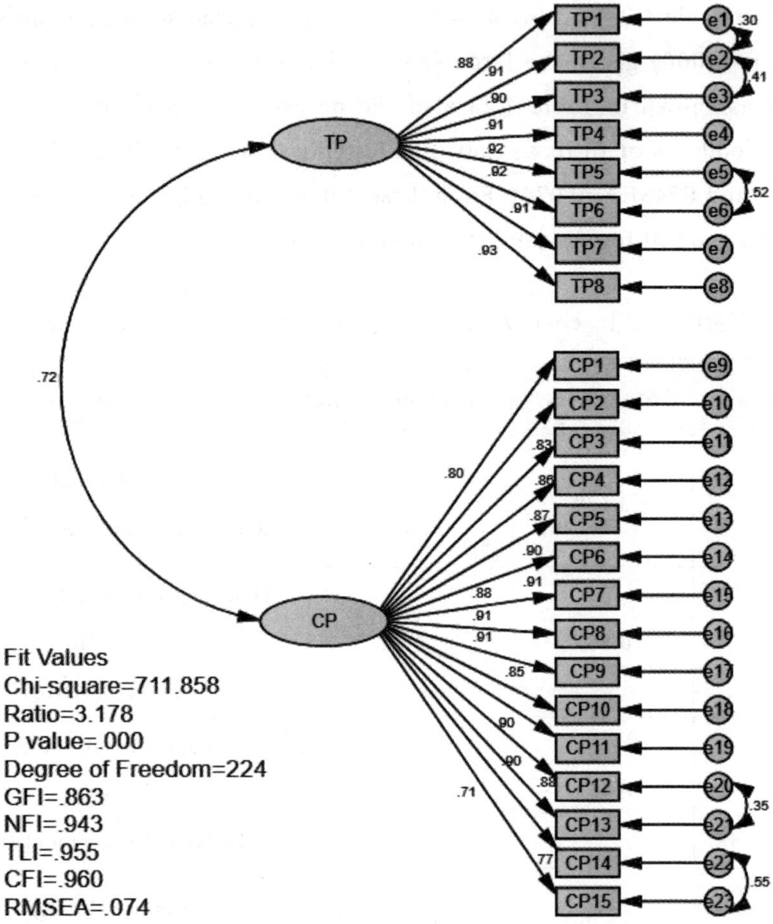

Figure 4.8. CFA for Construct of Job Performance

4.7.3.2. Discriminant Validity

Another main component of constructing validity is the discriminant validity. Discriminant validity is another proof of construct validity, which means that when different methods are applied to measure different constructs, the observed values should be distinguishable. In other words, it means that items should correlate higher among them than correlating with other types of items from other types of constructs that are theoretically supposed not to correlate (Zait and Bertea, 2011). In order to ensure discriminant validity, average variance extracted (AVE) is needed. If a measurement instrument has discriminant validity, the correlation between different constructs cannot be too strong. There are several ways to determine the discriminant validity between latent variables. This study refers to the study of Formell and Larcker (1981) by comparing the correlation coefficient between different variables in the measuring instrument with the AVE square root of each of the two variables. If the correlation coefficient between the two variables is less than the AVE square root of the two variables, the measuring instrument is considered to have good discriminant validity.

Table 4.24 shows the values of AVE for all latent variables. The values range between 0.66 and 0.83, which are higher than the recommended value (Fornell and Larcker, 1981). Besides, according to the statement of Byrne (2010), if the value of AVE is more than 0.50, it should be considered as an indication that discriminant validity exists amongst each latent variables in the proposed model.

Table 4.24 *Average Variance Extracted (AVE) of Latent Variables*

Variables	Items	AVE
Working Support	10	0.693
Identifying Value	7	0.658
Caring about Well-being	7	0.678
Vigor	3	0.659
Dedication	3	0.680
Absorption	3	0.642
Task Performance	8	0.829
Contextual Performance	15	0.739

After calculating the values of AVE of each latent variable, the whole measurement instrument is tested to obtain the correlation coefficient between the latent variables and the AVE square root of each latent variable. As can be seen from Table 4.25 below, the correlation coefficient of each row and each column is smaller than the square root value of the corresponding latent variable AVE, which indicates that the perceived organizational support scale has acceptable discriminant validity in the study.

Table 4.25 *Comparison between Square Root of each AVE and Correlation Coefficient for all Latent Variables*

Exogenous Variables	WS	IV	CW	VI	DE	AB	TP	CP
WS	0.832							
IV	.512**	0.811						
CW	.434**	.443**	0.823					
VI	.453**	.391**	.428**	0.812				
DE	.454**	.471**	.399**	.541**	0.825			
AB	.496**	.428**	.440**	.485**	.591**	0.801		
TP	.402**	.535**	.447**	.510**	.547**	.512**	0.910	
CP	.482**	.505**	.453**	.516**	.578**	.532**	.698**	0.860

**Significant at level of 0.01

Note: WS = Working Support, IV = Identifying Value, CW = Caring about Well-being, VI = Vigor, DE = Dedication, AB = Absorption, TP = Task Performance, CP = Contextual Performance

4.7.3.3 Composite Reliability

Composite Reliability (CR) refers to the extent to which the items consistently represent the same latent construct (Hair et al., 2010). Normally, the acceptable threshold for composite reliability is 0.70, which means, if the values of CR of each variable are higher than 0.70, the composite reliability is acceptable.

From the results shown in Table 4.26, it can be seen that all latent variables generally show an acceptable level of composite reliability with CR values ranging between 0.843 and 0.977, which are all more than 0.70. The results reveal a high level of consistency among items of each latent variable, and further confirm the good fit of the data for the measurement in the study.

Table 4.26 *Composite Reliability (CR) of Latent Variables*

Variables	Items	CR	AVE
Working Support	10	0.958	0.693
Identifying Value	7	0.931	0.658
Caring about Well-being	7	0.936	0.678
Vigor	3	0.852	0.659
Dedication	3	0.864	0.680
Absorption	3	0.843	0.642
Task Performance	8	0.975	0.829
Contextual Performance	15	0.977	0.739

4.8 Hypothesized Structural Model

After testing the goodness of the measurement instrument, the hypothesized model was produced based on the suggestion of modification indices to achieve a good fit for the data (Hair et al., 2010).

The model modification was conducted to improve the goodness of fit indices for the structural models. Since the present study aimed to test the relationship among perceived organizational support, work engagement and job performance, and also aimed to determine the relationship among dimensions of perceived organizational support (working support, identifying value and caring about well-being), dimensions of work engagement (vigor, dedication and absorption), and dimensions of work engagement (task performance and contextual performance), two structural models were generated to verify the hypotheses. This procedure would make it easier to examine the relationship among second-order constructs and the relationship among first-order constructs by constructing the models in such a way to test a total of 43 hypotheses in the study.

The second-order structural model was produced first with the goodness-of-fit indices. Table 4.27 shows that the ratio (CMIN/DF) is equal to 1.638, which is lower than the threshold value of 5. Other values (e.g. GFI=0.821, NFI=0.901, IFI=0.959, TLI=0.957, CFI=0.959) also could achieve the recommended cut-off values of model fit. Furthermore, the value of RMSEA (0.040) also represents the goodness of fit for the structural model.

More details are shown in Figure 4.9 and Table 4.27. Although the value of GFI does not exceed 0.9 and it is not high enough, it is still acceptable (Hair et al., 2010). And the values of the ratio, CFI, NFI, IFI, TLI, and RMSEA are both satisfactory. Thereby, it can be concluded that the second-order structural model has achieved the goodness of fit as shown by the indices. This structural model is suitable for study hypotheses testing.

Table 4.27 *Good-Fit-Indices of The Second-Order Structural Model*

Measures	Fit indices	Threshold Values	Source
Ratio	1.638	≤ 5	Marsh and Hocevar (1985); Schumacker and Lomax (2004)
GFI	0.821	≥ 0.8	Greenspoon and Saklofske (1998); Hair et al. (2010)
NFI	0.901	≥ 0.8	Greenspoon and Saklofske (1998); Forza and Filippini (1998)
IFI	0.959	≥ 0.9	Bentler (1990); Hair et al. (2010)
CFI	0.959	≥ 0.9	Bentler (1990); Hair et al. (2010)
TLI	0.957	≥ 0.9	Hair et al. (2010); Awang (2012)
RMSEA	0.040	≤ 0.08	Greenspoon and Saklofske (1998); Byrne (2001); Awang (2012)

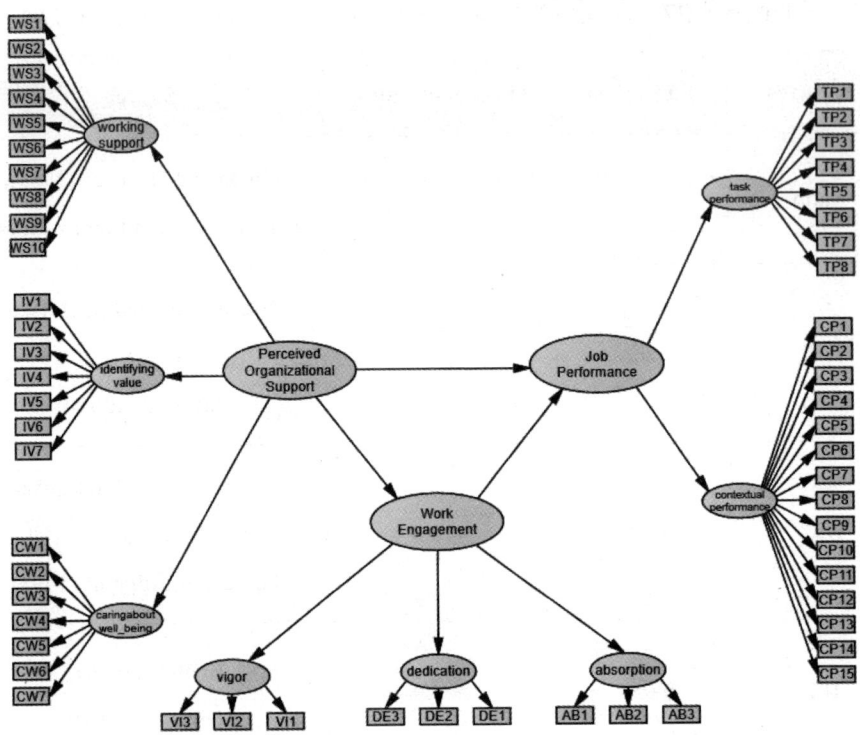

Figure 4.9. The Second–Order Structural Model

The first-order structural model was then produced with the goodness-of-fit indices. Table 4.28 shows that the ratio (CMIN/DF) is equal to 1.658, which is far lower than the threshold value of 5. Other values (e.g. GFI=0.824, NFI=0.901, IFI=0.958, TLI=0.955, CFI=0.958) also could achieve the recommended cut-off values of model fit. Furthermore, the value of RMSEA (0.041) also represents goodness of fit for the structural model. More details are shown in Figure 4.10 and Table 4.28. Although the value of GFI is not high enough, it is still acceptable (Hair et al., 2010). In addition, the values of the ratio, CFI, IFI, NFI, TLI and RMSEA are both satisfactory. Therefore, it can be concluded that the first-order structural model also has achieved the goodness of fit as showed by the indices. This structural model is suitable for study hypotheses testing.

Table 4.28 *Good-Fit-Indices of The First-Order Structural Model*

Measures	Fit indices	Threshold Values	Source
Ratio	1.658	≤ 5	Marsh and Hocevar (1985); Schumacker and Lomax (2004)
GFI	0.824	≥ 0.8	Greenspoon and Saklofske (1998); Hair et al. (2010)
NFI	0.901	≥ 0.8	Greenspoon and Saklofske (1998); Forza and Filippini (1998)
IFI	0.958	≥ 0.9	Bentler (1990); Hair et al. (2010)
CFI	0.958	≥ 0.9	Bentler (1990); Hair et al. (2010)
TLI	0.955	≥ 0.9	Hair et al. (2010); Awang (2012)
RMSEA	0.041	≤ 0.08	Greenspoon and Saklofske (1998); Byrne (2001); Awang (2012)

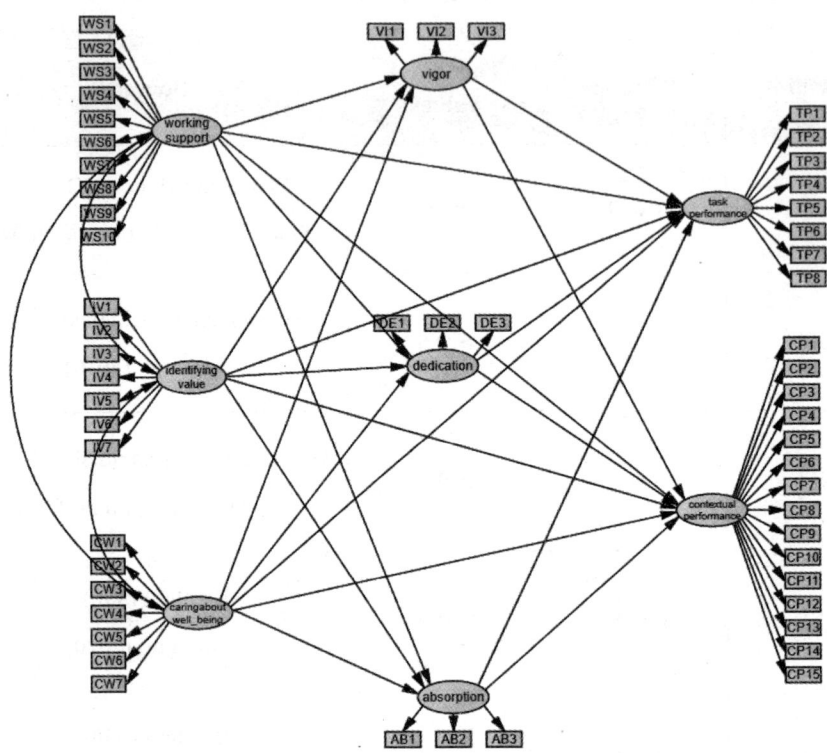

Figure 4.10. The First-Order Structural Model

4.9 Hypotheses Test

4.9.1 Direct Hypothesis Results

Hypotheses test was conducted based on the structural models presented as Figure 4.9 and 4.10. The hypotheses results are shown below:

1. Direct hypothesis results of the second-order structural model

For direct hypotheses test, the following three hypotheses were examined based on the second-order structural model:

H1: Perceived organizational support is positively related to job performance of grassroots administrative staff in newly-established universities.

H2: Perceived organizational support is positively related to work on engagement of grassroots administrative staff in newly-established universities.

H3: Work engagement is positively related to job performance of grassroots administrative staff in newly-established universities.

Table 4.29 which is presented below indicates the results of direct hypotheses between second-order constructs.

The results presented in Table 4.29 illustrate that perceived organizational support has a significant positive effect on job performance ($\beta=0.301$, $p<0.05$). In the same way, perceived organizational support has a significant positive effect on work engagement ($\beta=0.866$, $p<0.05$), work engagement has a significant positive effect on job performance (($\beta=0.600$, $p<0.05$). Therefore, hypotheses 1—3 are all accepted.

Table 4.29 *Direct Hypotheses Testing Result*

Hypotheses	Relationship	Std. Estimate	S.E.	C.R.	P
H1	Perceived Organizational Support → Job Performance	0.301	0.217	2.076	0.038
H2	Perceived Organizational Support → Work Engagement	0.866	0.089	9.306	***
H3	Work Engagement → Job Performance	0.600	0.233	4.050	***

***Significant at a level of 0.001.

Furthermore, squared multiple correlation (SMC) indicating the coefficient determination (R^2) is used in order to determine the total of the variance explained in endogenous variables by exogenous variables (Albright and Park, 2009). In AMOS model, the SMC shows the percentage of the variance in the dependent variable that the independent variables explain collectively. Table 4.30 indicates that the variable of perceived organizational support explained 75% of the variance in the variable of work engagement. For job performance, the results indicate that 76.4% of the variance of this dependent variable is explained by the variable of perceived organizational support and job performance.

Table 4.30 *Squared Multiple Correlation Results*

Endogenous Variables	Estimate SMC(R^2)
Work Engagement	0.750
Job Performance	0.764

2. Direct hypothesis results of the first-order structural model

For direct hypotheses test, the following twenty-one hypotheses were examined based on the first-order structural model:

H1.1: Working support is positively related to task performance.

H1.2: Working support is positively related to contextual performance.

H1.3: Identifying value is positively related to task performance.

H1.4: Identifying value is positively related to contextual performance.

H1.5: Caring about well-being is positively related to task performance.

H1.6: Caring about well-being is positively related to contextual performance.

H2.1: Working support is positively related to vigor.

H2.2: Working support is positively related to dedication.

H2.3: Working support is positively related to absorption.

H2.4: Identifying value is positively related to vigor.

H2.5: Identifying value is positively related to dedication.

H2.6: Identifying value is positively related to absorption.

H2.7: Caring about well-being is positively related to vigor.

H2.8: Caring about well-being is positively related to dedication.

H2.9 Caring about well-being is positively related to absorption.

H3.1: Vigor is positively related to task performance.

H3.2: Vigor is positively related to contextual performance.

H3.3: Dedication is positively related to task performance.

H3.4: Dedication is positively related to contextual performance.

H3.5: Absorption is positively related to task performance.

H3.6: Absorption is positively related to contextual performance.

The results presented in Table 4.31 indicate that most of direct hypotheses are supported, including H1.3 (identifying value → task performance), H1.4 (identifying value→ contextual performance), H2.1 (working support → vigor), H2.2 (working support → dedication), H2.3 (working support →absorption), H2.4 (identifying value → vigor), H2.5 (identifying value → dedication), H2.6 (identifying value → absorption), H2.7 (caring about well-being → vigor), H2.8 (caring about well-being → dedication), H2.9 (caring about well-being → absorption), H3.1 (vigor → task performance), H3.2 (vigor → contextual performance), H3.3 (dedication → task performance), H3.4 (dedication → contextual performance), H3.5 (absorption → task performance), H3.6 (absorption → contextual performance). The values of the standard estimate of them are all positive, and the p-value is all less than 0.05, which means that the effect is significant.

However, H1.1 is not supported because the effect of working support on task performane ($\beta=-0.135$, $p=0.155$) is not significant, and the value of the beta coefficient is negative. Similarly, H1.2($\beta=0.029$, $p=0.642$) which hypothesizes that working support has a positive impact on contextual performance, H1.5($\beta=0.104$, $p=0.105$) which hypothesizes that caring about well-being has a positive effect on task performance, and H1.6($\beta=0.077$, $p=0.183$) which hypothesizes that caring about well-being has a positive impact on contextual performance are all rejected because their p-values are greater than 0.05.

Table 4.31   *Direct Hypotheses Testing Result*

Hypotheses	Relationship	Estimate	Std. Estimate	S.E.	C.R.	P
H1.1	Working Support → Task Performance	−0.135	−0.109	0.070	−1.923	0.155
H1.2	Working Support → Contextual Performance	0.029	0.026	0.063	0.464	0.642
H1.3	Identifying Value → Task Performance	0.320	0.267	0.067	4.768	***
H1.4	Identifying Value → Contextual Performance	0.180	0.164	0.060	3.024	0.002
H1.5	Caring about well-being → Task Performance	0.104	0.086	0.064	1.623	0.105
H1.6	Caring about well-being → Contextual Performance	0.077	0.069	0.058	1.331	0.183
H2.1	Working Support → Vigor	0.275	0.303	0.055	5.009	***
H2.2	Working Support → Dedication	0.238	0.244	0.057	4.167	***
H2.3	Working Support → Absorption	0.352	0.338	0.062	5.673	***
H2.4	Identifying Value → Vigor	0.139	0.157	0.054	2.592	0.010
H2.5	Identifying Value → Dedication	0.295	0.311	0.058	5.134	***

Continued

Hypotheses	Relationship	Estimate	Std. Estimate	S.E.	C.R.	P
H2.6	Identifying Value→ Absorption	0.187	0.184	0.060	3.100	0.002
H2.7	Caring about well-being→ Vigor	0.245	0.274	0.052	4.746	***
H2.8	Caring about well-being→ Dedication	0.193	0.202	0.054	3.610	***
H2.9	Caring about well-being→ Absorption	0.266	0.259	0.058	4.600	***
H3.1	Vigor→ Task Performance	0.333	0.246	0.073	4.534	***
H3.2	Vigor→ Contextual Performance	0.282	0.228	0.066	4.278	***
H3.3	Dedication→ Task Performance	0.300	0.237	0.070	4.305	***
H3.4	Dedication→ Contextual Performance	0.324	0.280	0.064	5.093	***
H3.5	Absorption→ Task Performance	0.234	0.198	0.068	3.468	***
H3.6	Absorption→ Contextual Performance	0.204	0.188	0.061	3.363	***

***Significant at a level of 0.001.

Furthermore, squared multiple correlation (SMC) which indicates the coefficient determination (R^2) is used in order to determine the total of the variance explained in endogenous variables by exogenous variables (Albright and Park, 2009).

Table 4.32 indicates that the three exogenous variables (working support, identifying value and caring about well-being) collectively explained 40.9% of the variance in absorption. Similarly, these three independent variables jointly explained 38.4% of the variance in dedication, and together explained 35.9% of the variance in vigor.

As for contextual performance, the results indicate that 51.3% of the variance of this dependent variable is explained collectively by working support, identifying value, caring about well-being, vigor, dedication and absorption. Furthermore, 50.0% of the variance of task performance is also explained by these six variables.

Table 4.32 *Squared Multiple Correlation Results*

Endogenous Variables	Estimate SMC(R^2)
Absorption	0.409
Dedication	0.384
Vigor	0.359
Contextual Performance	0.513
Task Performance	0.500

4.9.2 Indirect Hypothesis Results: Testing the Mediating Effect

This study aims to test the mediating effect of work engagement between perceived organizational support and job performance. The mediating effect of dimensions of work engagement, namely, working support, identifying value and caring about well-being, is also tested.

According to the suggestion of Preacher and Hays (2008), bootstrapping procedure was utilized to determine the existence of significant pathways between independent variables and dependent variables via work engagement as mediator. In order to realize it, new samples (with replacement) were extracted from the sample 1,000 times and all the direct and indirect effects of the structural model were calculated. At the same time, bias-corrected confidence intervals were reported at 95% level of confidence (Preacher and Hays, 2008).

Compared to other frequently used techniques such as the Sobel test and the causal steps strategy, bootstrapping is one of the most valid and powerful method for testing intervening variable effects and computes higher accurate confidence intervals (CI) for indirect effects (Baron and Kenny, 1986; Mackinnon, Lockwood, and Williams, 2004).

To investigate the mediating effect of work engagement (second-order construct) and its dimensions (first-order constructs), direct and indirect estimated values of the structural model were calculated first by AMOS (Preacher and Hays, 2008). Then, the mediating effect is determined according to the following rules: if the significance of indirect effect is lower than 0.05, or in other words, if there is no zero between the values of the lower bound and upper bound, it is considered that mediating effect exists. To determine whether it is a full mediation or a partial mediation, the indirect effect and direct effect both need to be observed. If the indirect effect is significant ($p < 0.05$), or if the indirect effect's 95% confidence intervals (from lower bound to upper bound) do not include zero, but the direct effect is not significant ($p > 0.05$), namely, there is a zero between the lower bound and the upper bound, then this indirect effect can be considered as full mediation. On the other hand, in the case where the indirect effect is significant, the direct effect is also significant, but its value is lower than the total effect, it can be considered as a partial mediation (Zainudin, 2014).

1. Mediating effect analysis of the second-order structural model

For indirect hypotheses test, the following hypothesis was examined first by the bootstrapping method:

H4: Work engagement has a positive mediating effect in the relationship between perceived organizational support and job performance of grassroots administrative staff in newly-established universities.

The bootstrapping result presented in Table 4.33 reveals that the relationship between perceived organizational support and job performance is fully mediated by work engagement since the indirect effect is significant, and the direct effect is not significant.

Table 4.33 *Result of Mediation of Work Engagement*

Hypothesis	Relationships	Point Estimate	95% CI Lower	95% CI Upper	Result of Effect	Result
H4	POS → JP	0.451	-0.195	1.005	Direct effect is not significant	Full mediation
	POS → WE → JP	0.779	0.396	1.386	Indirect effect is significant	

Note: POS=Perceived Organizational Support, WE=Work Engagement, JP=Job Performance.

2. Mediating effect analysis of the first-order structural model

In the past, scholars' research on mediating effects mainly focused on a single mediator variable. This mediating effect is called simple mediation. In fact, there are also multiple mediating variables that mediate collectively the relationship between the independent variable and the dependent variable. These mediating effects are called multiple-mediator modeling (Liu and Ling, 2009).

In the field of social science research, research is complex and often requires multiple mediator variables to more clearly explain the effects of independent variables on dependent variables (Mackinnon, 2008). In recent years, more and more research on mediation has begun to adopt multiple mediation models. However, most studies just disassembled multiple mediation models into several simple models, that is, only one mediator in one model, and then performed several simple mediation analyses (Fang, et al., 2014). This study constructed a multiple mediation structure model (Figure 4.10) for multi-mediator analysis, which can analyze the relationship between multiple independent variables, multiple dependent variables and multiple mediating variables at the same time and same model, which is a better method.

In multiple mediation structural equation model, the most important type of effect for assessing mediation is the specific indirect effect (Brown, 1997). Particularly, specific indirect effect represents the portion of the total indirect effect than work through a single intervening variable (Holbert and Stephenson, 2003).

For multiple mediators, Amos cannot directly estimate the statistical significance of specific indirect effects. Therefore, PRODCLIN (distribution of the PRODuct Confidence Limits for INdirect effects), which is a program computing confidence limits for the product of two normal random variables, is utilized by the researcher in this study. According to Mackinnon, Fritz, William and Lockwood (2007), PRODCLIN can be used to obtain more accurate confidence limits for the indirect effects.

For specific indirect hypotheses test, the following 18 hypotheses would be examined by PRODCLIN program:

H4.1: Vigor has a positive mediating effect in the relationship between working support and task performance.

H4.2: Vigor has a positive mediating effect in the relationship between working support and contextual performance.

H4.3: Vigor has a positive mediating effect in the relationship between identifying value and task performance.

H4.4: Vigor has a positive mediating effect in the relationship between identifying value and contextual performance.

H4.5: Vigor has a positive mediating effect in the relationship between caring about well-being and task performance.

H4.6: Vigor has a positive mediating effect in the relationship between caring about well-being and contextual performance.

H4.7: Dedication has a positive mediating effect in the relationship between working support and task performance.

H4.8: Dedication has a positive mediating effect in the relationship between working support and contextual performance.

H4.9: Dedication has a positive mediating effect in the relationship between identifying value and task performance.

H4.10: Dedication has a positive mediating effect in the relationship between identifying value and contextual performance.

H4.11: Dedication has a positive mediating effect in the relationship between caring about well-being and task performance.

H4.12: Dedication has a positive mediating effect in the relationship between caring about well-being and contextual performance.

H4.13: Absorption has a positive mediating effect in the relationship between working support and task performance.

H4.14: Absorption has a positive mediating effect in the relationship between working support and contextual performance.

H4.15: Absorption has a positive mediating effect in the relationship between identifying value and task performance.

H4.16: Absorption has a positive mediating effect in the relationship between identifying value and contextual performance.

H4.17: Absorption has a positive mediating effect in the relationship between caring about well-being and task performance.

H4.18: Absorption has a positive mediating effect in the relationship between caring about well-being and contextual performance.

Based on the analysis of the structural model of the multiple mediation and the operation of the PRODCLIN program, the final results of the multiple mediation are derived and shown in Table 4.34. As can be seen from the table, all of the three mediator variables (vigor, dedication and absorption) have indirect effects among three independent variables (working support, identifying value and caring about well-being) and two dependent variables (task performance and contextual performance).

The point estimates for these specific indirect effects are all positive, and their 95% confidence intervals (from lower bound to upper bound) contain no zeros, so it can be confirmed that three mediator variables (vigor, dedication, and absorption) positively mediate the relationship between independent variables (working support, identifying value and caring about well-being) and dependent variables (task performance and contextual performance).

Among these 18 mediation hypotheses, the indirect effects in H4.1, H4.2, H4.5, H4.6, H4.7, H4.8, H4.11, H4.12, H4.13, H4.14, H4.17, H4.18 are significant and positive, but the direct effects are insignificant, hence the mediators in these hypotheses can be considered as full mediation. On the contrary, the indirect effects in

H4.3, H4.4, H4.9, H4.10, H4.15, H4.16 are significant and positive, while the direct effects are significant and positive. Therefore, the mediators in these hypotheses can be considered as partial mediation. More details are presented in Table 4.34 below.

So far, all 24 direct effect hypotheses and 19 indirect effects of this study have been tested.

Table 4.34 *Results of Multiple Mediators (Vigor, Dedication, Absorption)*

Hypothesis	Relationships	Point Estimate	95% CI Lower	95% CI Upper	Result of Effect	Result
H4.1	WS → TP	−0.135	−0.262	0.005	Direct effect is not significant	Full mediation
	WS → VI → TP	0.092	0.042	0.154	Indirect effect is significant	
H4.2	WS → CP	0.029	−0.091	0.164	Direct effect is not significant	Full mediation
	WS → VI → CP	0.078	0.033	0.137	Indirect effect is significant	
H4.3	IV → TP	0.320	0.197	0.449	Direct effect is significant	Partial mediation
	IV → VI → TP	0.046	0.008	0.103	Indirect effect is significant	
H4.4	IV → CP	0.180	0.056	0.300	Direct effect is significant	Partial mediation
	IV → VI → CP	0.039	0.007	0.086	Indirect effect is significant	
H4.5	CW → TP	0.104	−0.042	0.234	Direct effect is not significant	Full mediation
	CW → VI → TP	0.082	0.035	0.144	Indirect effect is significant	

Continued

Hypothesis	Relationships	Point Estimate	95% CI Lower	95% CI Upper	Result of Effect	Result
H4.6	CW → CP	0.077	−0.063	0.193	Direct effect is not significant	Full mediation
	CW → VI → CP	0.069	0.028	0.124	Indirect effect is significant	
H4.7	WS → TP	−0.135	−0.262	0.005	Direct effect is not significant	Full mediation
	WS → DE → TP	0.071	0.029	0.127	Indirect effect is significant	
H4.8	WS → CP	0.029	−0.091	0.164	Direct effect is not significant	Full mediation
	WS → DE → CP	0.077	0.041	0.171	Indirect effect is significant	
H4.9	IV → TP	0.320	0.197	0.449	Direct effect is significant	Partial mediation
	IV → DE → TP	0.089	0.035	0.161	Indirect effect is significant	
H4.10	IV → CP	0.180	0.056	0.300	Direct effect is significant	Partial mediation
	IV → DE → CP	0.096	0.044	0.164	Indirect effect is significant	
H4.11	CW → TP	0.104	−0.042	0.234	Direct effect is not significant	Full mediation
	CW → DE → TP	0.058	0.019	0.112	Indirect effect is significant	

Continued

Hypothesis	Relationships	Point Estimate	95% CI Lower	95% CI Upper	Result of Effect	Result
H4.12	CW → CP	0.077	−0.063	0.193	Direct effect is not significant	Full mediation
	CW → DE → CP	0.063	0.023	0.116	Indirect effect is significant	
H4.13	WS → TP	−0.135	−0.262	0.005	Direct effect is not significant	Full mediation
	WS → AB → TP	0.082	0.031	0.146	Indirect effect is significant	
H4.14	WS → CP	0.029	−0.091	0.164	Direct effect is not significant	Full mediation
	WS → AB → CP	0.072	0.025	0.133	Indirect effect is significant	
H4.15	IV → TP	0.320	0.197	0.449	Direct effect is significant	Partial mediation
	IV → AB → TP	0.044	0.009	0.098	Indirect effect is significant	
H4.16	IV → CP	0.180	0.056	0.300	Direct effect is significant	Partial mediation
	IV → AB → CP	0.038	0.008	0.084	Indirect effect is significant	
H4.17	CW → TP	0.104	−0.042	0.234	Direct effect is not significant	Full mediation
	CW → AB → TP	0.062	0.020	0.120	Indirect effect is significant	

Continued

Hypothesis	Relationships	Point Estimate	95% CI		Result of Effect	Result
			Lower	Upper		
H4.18	CW → CP	0.077	−0.063	0.193	Direct effect is not significant	Full mediation
	CW → AB → CP	0.054	0.017	0.105	Indirect effect is significant	

Note: WS=Working Support, IV= Identifying Value, CW= Caring about Well-being, VI=Vigor, DE=Dedication, AB=Absorption, TP=Task Performance, CP=Contextual Performance

4.9.3 Conclusion of Hypotheses Test

Based on relevant theories and previous studies, this study proposes four main hypotheses and 39 underlying hypotheses. In order to test the hypotheses of the study, two structural models were built. One is used to determine the modeling relationship among second-order constructs including perceived organizational support, work engagement and job performance. The other one is used to analyze the modeling relationship among first-order constructs including working support, identifying value, caring about well-being, vigor, dedication, absorption, task performance and contextual performance. Most of the hypotheses of the study were accepted, whereas four hypotheses were denied. For ease of reviewing, all hypotheses testing results are organized into the following table.

Table 4.35 *All Hypotheses Testing Results*

Research Hypotheses	Results
H1 Perceived organizational support is positively related to job performance	Supported
H1.1 Working support is positively related to task performance	Rejected
H1.2 Working support is positively related to contextual performance	Rejected
H1.3 Identifying value is positively related to task performance	Supported

Continued

Research Hypotheses	Results
H1.4　Identifying value is positively related to contextual performance	Supported
H1.5　Caring about well-being is positively related to task performance	Rejected
H1.6　Caring about well-being is positively related to contextual performance	Rejected
H2: Perceived organizational support is positively related to work engagement	Supported
H2.1 Working support is positively related to vigor	Supported
H2.2 Working support is positively related to dedication	Supported
H2.3 Working support is positively related to absorption	Supported
H2.4 Identifying value is positively related to vigor	Supported
H2.5 Identifying value is positively related to dedication	Supported
H2.6 Identifying value is positively related to absorption.	Supported
H2.7 Caring about well-being is positively related to vigor	Supported
H2.8 Caring about well-being is positively related to dedication	Supported
H2.9 Caring about well-being is positively related to absorption	Supported
H3 Work engagement is positively related to job performance	Supported
H3.1 Vigor is positively related to task performance	Supported
H3.2 Vigor is positively related to contextual performance	Supported
H3.3 Dedication is positively related to task performance	Supported
H3.4 Dedication is positively related to contextual performance	Supported
H3.5 Absorption is positively related to task performance	Supported
H3.6 Absorption is positively related to contextual performance	Supported
H4 Engagement has a positive mediating effect in the relationship between perceived organizational support and job performance	Supported

Continued

Research Hypotheses	Results
H4.1 Vigor has a positive mediating effect in the relationship between working support and task performance	Supported
H4.2 Vigor has a positive mediating effect in the relationship between working support and contextual performance	Supported
H4.3 Vigor has a positive mediating effect in the relationship between identifying value and task performance	Supported
H4.4 Vigor has a positive mediating effect in the relationship between identifying value and contextual performance	Supported
H4.5 Vigor has a positive mediating effect in the relationship between caring about well-being and task performance	Supported
H4.6 Vigor has a positive mediating effect in the relationship between caring about well-being and contextual performance	Supported
H4.7 Dedication has a positive mediating effect in the relationship between working support and task performance	Supported
H4.8 Dedication has a positive mediating effect in the relationship between working support and contextual performance	Supported
H4.9 Dedication has a positive mediating effect in the relationship between identifying value and task performance	Supported
H4.10 Dedication has a positive mediating effect in the relationship between identifying value and contextual performance	Supported
H4.11 Dedication has a positive mediating effect in the relationship between caring about well-being and task performance	Supported
H4.12 Dedication has a positive mediating effect in the relationship between caring about well-being and contextual performance	Supported
H4.13 Absorption has a positive mediating effect in the relationship between working support and task performance	Supported

Continued

Research Hypotheses	Results
H4.14 Absorption has a positive mediating effect in the relationship between working support and contextual performance	Supported
H4.15 Absorption has a positive mediating effect in the relationship between identifying value and task performance	Supported
H4.16 Absorption has a positive mediating effect in the relationship between identifying value and contextual performance	Supported
H4.17 Absorption has a positive mediating effect in the relationship between caring about well-being and task performance	Supported
H4.18 Absorption has a positive mediating effect in the relationship between caring about well-being and contextual performance	Supported

4.10 Summary

In this chapter, all of the research questions have been addressed by several analyses based on data collected in the study. It should be noted that the generated structural models in this study maintained the original constructs and the respective items of each individual construct, because factor loadings of all retained items are above the threshold of 0.50 and the goodness of fit of construct model is acceptable.

Additionally, the first-order and second-order structural models were developed after modification and achieving the goodness of fit indices. The research hypotheses were all tested and the relationships among the research variables were determined. Particularly, mediation results which complicated are shown in the last section. The results show that out of 44 hypotheses, 40 hypotheses are accepted whereas four hypotheses are rejected. In other words, the results in general accept most of the hypotheses. These results are furthermore discussed in greater details in the final chapter.

CHAPTER FIVE: DISCUSSION AND CONCLUSION

5.1 Introduction

The final chapter of this thesis first recapitulates the research findings and then goes on to provides a more detailed discussion of the findings presented in Chapter 4 with reference to the proposed hypotheses. The study adopts a quantitative method research design where the data collected are analyzed to answer five research questions. This chapter offers recommendations on how to improve the job performance of university administrative staff based on the discussion of findings. In addition, the final part of this chapter discusses future research directions.

5.2 Recapitulations of Research Findings

This study works to contribute to the understanding of whether or not the effect of different perceived organizational support on job performance may be reflective of the nature of work engagement in the Chinese context. Thus, the issue is whether or not engagement mediates the impact of perceived organizational support on job performance. More specifically, the objectives of this study are:

1. To determine the level of perceived organizational support, engagement and job performance of grassroots administrative staff in newly-established universities

in Sichuan, China.

2. To examine whether perceived organizational support influences job performance of grassroots administrative staff in newly-established universities in Sichuan, China.

3. To identify whether perceived organizational support influences engagement of grassroots administrative staff in newly-established universities in Sichuan, China.

4. To investigate whether engagement influences job performance of grassroots administrative staff in newly-established universities in Sichuan, China.

5. To determine the mediating role of engagement between perceived organizational support and job performance of grassroots administrative staff in newly-established universities in Sichuan, China.

In this study, perceived organizational support is examined through working support, identifying value and caring about well-being. Work engagement is measured on vigor, dedication and absorption. Furthermore, job performance is examined on task performance and contextual performance. The research questions are addressed using a quantitative approach where questionnaires composed of perceived organizational support scale, work engagement scale and job performance scale were distributed to sample administrative staff from sampled newly-established universities in Sichuan province, China.

Literature is reviewed and as reported in Chapter 2 the theoretical framework is employed to describe the relationship between research constructs. Based on relevant theories and previous research, four main hypotheses and 39 underlying hypotheses are proposed and tested.

In order to address the research questions and examine the hypotheses, SPSS and AMOS are utilized in the study. SPSS is used to conduct a preliminary data analysis, such as detection of outliers, a test of normality, a test of common method variance, a test of non-response bias, descriptive analysis, a test of reliability and EFA. AMOS is used to build structural models for confirmatory factor analysis and hypotheses test. The results show that there is a low level of perceived organizational support, work engagement and job performance among administrative staff in newly-established universities. It also reveals that there are positive relationships among perceive organizational support, work engagement and job performance. Besides, work engagement can mediate between perceiving organizational support and job performance.

5.3 Discussions of Research Findings

This section is the discussions of research findings which are in line with the research questions raised in the study. This section entails the discussion on the level of perceived organizational support, work engagement and job performance of administrative staff in newly-established universities of China, the impact of each variable as well as the mediating effect of work engagement.

5.3.1 Research Question 1

What is the level of perceived organizational support, engagement and job performance of grassroots administrative staff in newly-established universities in Sichuan, China?

The job performance of grassroots administrative staff in newly-established universities is the dependent variable in this study with two dimensions, including task performance and job performance. As showed in the analysis of data collected for the study, the mean values of the two dimensions by using 5-Likert scales ranged from 2.50 to 2.54. The mean value justifies that the level of job performance of grassroots administrative staff is lower than 3 points which is the middle value of the 5-Likert scale. It reveals that grassroots administrative staff has a slightly low level of job performance. This result is consistent with the view of many researchers that university administrative staff has low job performance (Dong and Ma, 2013; Gao, 2015; Si, 2010; Yang, 2017; Yu, Liu and Liu, 2013).

This outcome probably suggests that the government, higher education management authorities and university management levels in China, particularly in Sichuan province, should try to find effective ways to enhance administrative staff's job performance, which can affect university administration level, and eventually even the quality of higher education.

CHAPTER FIVE : DISCUSSION AND CONCLUSION

The findings also indicate that Chinese university grassroots administrative staff showed a moderate and low level of perceived organizational support. Compared with the mean values of job performance, the level of perceived organizational support (2.78) is a little higher, but still below the intermediate value of 3 points. In three dimensions of perception of organizational support, administrative staff feels a little stronger about caring about well-being (2.86) from the organization, while feeling less about working support (2.73) and identifying value (2.77) from the organization. These results reveal the status quo of administrative staff that is not valued and supported sufficiently by organizations in Chinese universities. This result is in support with the previous finding of Chen (2017) who found that administrative staff is at a low level of satisfaction with salary and organizational caring, that is, they do not think they received adequate support from the organization. The result also supports the viewpoint of Yu, Liu and Liu (2013) who elaborate that administrative staff, especially grassroots administrative staff is usually marginalized and do not receive sufficient support from the university. This result should probably be a reminder that in university management, attention should also be paid to the support for administrative staff while focusing on academic and teaching staff.

Furthermore, this study also reveals that the level of work engagement among university grassroots administrative staff is moderately low. In terms of dimensions of work engagement, the mean values of vigor, dedication, absorption are 2.70, 2.62, and 2.76 respectively. This result probably suggests that the government, higher education management authorities and university management levels in China should attempt to find more effective ways to motivate administrative staff's work engagement.

5.3.2 Research Question 2

Does perceive organizational support affect the job performance of grassroots administrative staff in newly-established universities in Sichuan, China?

The first hypothesis and its underlying hypotheses (from H1.1 to H1.6) formulated for this study are to address Research Question 2. The findings from Chapter 4 reveal that there is a positive relationship between perceiving organizational support and job performance among university administrative staff. In other words, perceived organizational support positively influences job performance. This conclusion is consistent with most of the previous studies focusing on the relationship between perceived organizational support and job performance (Afzali et al., 2014; Akgunduz and Sanli, 2017; Eisenberger et al., 2001; Kraimer and Wayne, 2004; Krishnan, 2016; Luo, 2014; Pearce and Herbik, 2004).

However, unlike the sample population of other related studies, this study uses university administrative staff as the target population for research. Hence there are some unique findings on the relationship between variables explaining perceived organizational support and job performance. Among the dimensions of perceived organizational support, identifying value can significantly affect task performance and contextual performance, whereas the effect of working support and caring about well-being on task performance and contextual performance is insignificant. It reveals that identifying value is more able to promote job performance among university administrative staff, compared with working support and caring about well-being. These findings probably suggest that the university should first let employees feel that their value is recognized by the organization when considering the support for employees.

5.3.3 Research Question 3

Does perceive organizational support affect work engagement of grassroots administrative staff in newly-established universities in Sichuan, China?

The second hypothesis and its underlying hypotheses (from H2.1 to H2.9) formulated for this study are to address Research Question 3. The findings of the study reveal that there is a positive relationship between perceived organizational support and work engagement among university administrative staff. In other words, perceived organizational support significantly influences work engagement. This conclusion is consistent with most of the previous studies focusing on the relationship between perceived organizational support and work engagement (Caesens and Stinglhamber, 2014; Chen and Zhang, 2010; Leiter and Laschinger, 2006; Rothmann and Joubert, 2007; Saks, 2006; Wang et al., 2017; Yang and Liao, 2009).

CHAPTER FIVE : DISCUSSION AND CONCLUSION

In terms of dimensions of perceived organizational support and work engagement, the findings indicate that working support, identifying value and caring about well-being all significantly affect the dimensions of work engagement (vigor, dedication and absorption). Furthermore, according to the suggestion of Albright and Park (2009), squared multiple correlation (SMC) is utilized to indicate the coefficient determination (R^2) in the study. The values of R^2 show that the three exogenous variables (working support, identifying value and caring about well-being) collectively explained 40.3% of the variance in absorption. Similarly, these three independent variables jointly explained 37.1% of the variance in dedication, and together explained 35.4% of the variance in vigor. Overall, 75.0% of the variance of work engagement is explained by the perceived organizational support. It reveals that work engagement may not only be predicted significantly by perceived organizational support, but also explained strongly by perceived organizational support.

5.3.4 Research Question 4

Does work engagement affect job performance of grassroots administrative staff in newly-established universities in Sichuan, China?

The third hypothesis and its underlying hypotheses (from H3.1 to H3.6) formulated for this study are to solve Research Question 4. Similar to the results of the previous two relationships, the findings also reveal that a positive relationship exists between work engagement and job performance of university administrative staff. This shows that work engagement significantly influences job performance. This is similar to the conclusions of many related research which studied the relationship between work engagement and job performance in different contexts and based on various target samples (Al-dalahmeh, Masa'deh, Abu Khalaf and Obeidat, 2018; Anitha, 2014; Bakker et al., 2015; Lawlor and Collins, 2017; Rich, 2010; Zhang, 2016).

In terms of dimensions of work engagement and job performance, the findings after data analysis shows that vigor, dedication and absorption all significantly affect the dimensions of job performance (task performance and contextual performance). It suggests that enhancing work engagement must be achieved in order to improve job performance among grassroots administrative staff in newly-established universities.

5.3.5 Research Question 5

Does work engagement mediate the relationship between perceived organizational support and job performance of grassroots administrative staff in newly-established universities in Sichuan, China?

In order to address the final research question, which is the most important question, the fourth hypothesis and its 18 underlying hypotheses (from H4.1 to H4.18) are proposed and then tested one by one using AMOS and PRODCLIN, which is a program computing confidence limits for the product of two normal random variables.

According to data analysis and findings in the previous chapter, all mediation hypotheses are accepted. That means, not only does work engagement play a mediating role between perceived organizational support and job performance, but the dimensions of work engagement also mediate between dimensions of perceived organizational support and work performance. To be more specific, vigor, dedication and absorption have full mediation effect between working support and task performance, and full mediation effect between working support and contextual performance, and full mediation effect between caring about well-being and task performance, and also full mediation effect between caring about well-being and contextual performance.

On the other hand, vigor, dedication and absorption have a partial mediation effect between identifying value and task performance, and full mediation effect between identifying value and contextual performance. It can be considered that among dimensions of perceived organizational support, working support and caring about well-being have indirect effects on job performance, which need work engagement (vigor, dedication and absorption) to mediate, whereas identifying value has a direct effect on job performance, which also can be mediated by work engagement.

Overall, the results of testing modeling relationship show that the organization's support for administrative staff can significantly affect their job performance. However, this influence requires work engagement, that is, administrative staff's vigor, dedication, and absorption to mediate, in order to act on their job performance. Therefore, it can be concluded that when providing organizational support for administrative staff, if cultivating and improving their work engagement can also be considered, the improvement of job performance will be more significant. Moreover, the findings reveal that identifying value is the most valuable and important among all observed variables in the modeling relationship, because identifying value not only have positive effect on vigor, dedication and absorption, but also positively impact task performance and contextual performance, whereas working support and caring about well-being only have indirect influence on task performance and contextual performance. It probably indicates that the grassroots administrative staff in newly-established universities prefer non-material support to material support from their universities, although material support is still important. In particular, the recognition of the value and the recognition of contributions, as an intangible support, can more motivate administrative staff to engage in work and improve job performance.

5.4 Contributions of the Study

By developing the research framework and testing the modeling relationship between perceived organizational support, work engagement and job performance, this research has added some contributions to both the academic and practical field. It provides several implications for higher education authorities and newly established university management. Besides, it can serve as a theoretical background for further research in the field of higher education management or human resource management.

5.4.1 Theoretical Contribution

This study contributes to the arts and sciences literature by providing more evidence of the relationship between perceived organizational support, work engagement and job performance. Although there are many researchers studying the effect of perceived organizational support or engagement on job performance, they seldom considered the mediating effect of work engagement. The study confirms that there is a significant positive relationship between three variables, and find that work engagement is a full mediation between perceived organizational support and job performance. Furthermore, relevant theories helping to construct the research framework, including JD-R theory, psychological contract theory, self-determination theory, the norm of reciprocity, attribution theory, social exchange theory have been proved again by this empirical study.

The outcome of this research contributes to filling an academic knowledge gap in the literature, which continuously elicits the need for further empirical research on perceived organizational support, engagement and job performance within diverse contexts and different target samples. It can be seen that related empirical research has involved business, medical, manufacturing, and tourism practitioners, but rarely involved the field of education management. In particular, researchers are less concerned about the administration of higher education institutions (Kivistö and Pekkola, 2017). As a special demographic group, university administrative staff in China which has become a veritable higher education country did not receive much attention. The level of perceived organizational support, engagement, and job performance of university administrative staff in the context of the rapid development of Chinese higher education is still unknown, and their relationship is uncertain. This study filled this academic gap.

This research enriches the current body of knowledge in perceived organizational support theory and relevant empirical study. According to a suggestion by Ling et al. (2006), the administrative staff's perception of organizational support is divided into working support, identifying value and caring about well-being in the context of Chinese culture. The findings of the study indicate that identifying value can be directly and indirectly impact job performance, while working support and caring about well-being just have an indirect effect on job performance which needs work engagement to play as a mediator role. They also reveal that the organization's recognition of the value of employees may be the most important among the organizational support, although perceived organizational support has been found to have important consequences to employee performance.

In addition, the dimensions and scales which are used to measure perceived organizational support, work engagement and job performance have been confirmed to be suitable for the study in the field of education management, and also in the oriental culture context, since they have been tested by EFA and confirmatory factor analysis (CFA) in the study. It provides evidence for wide applicability of dimensions and scales of these variables in the study.

5.4.2 Methodological Contribution

This study extends the framework of previous studies in which the role of work engagement as a mediator between perceived organizational support and job performance was considered to be limited. Hence, it has contributed through a complex research framework.

In particular, this thesis not only studies the relationships between three variables of perceived organizational support, work engagement and job performance, but also studies the relationships among first-order variables, including working support, identifying value, caring about well-being, vigor, dedication, absorption, task performance and contextual performance. The second-order structural model and the first-order structural model are built at the same time which can explore the relationship between variables more deeply, more clearly, more accurately, and in more detail.

Moreover, the use of multiple mediation analysis to test many indirect hypotheses through bootstrapping method and PRODCLIN program is also considered as a methodological contribution. In the past, scholars' research on mediating effects mainly focused on a single mediator variable, namely simple mediation (Liu and Ling, 2009). However, nowadays, research is complex and often requires multiple mediator variables to more clearly explain the effects of independent variables on dependent variables (Mackinnon, 2008). Although more research on mediation has begun to conduct multiple mediation analysis in recent years, they just disassembled a multiple mediation model into several simple models, and then performed several simple mediation analyses (Fang et al., 2014).

However, this study constructs a multiple mediation structure model (Figure 4.10) for multiple mediation analysis, which can analyze the relationship between multiple independent variables, multiple dependent variables and multiple mediator variables at the same time and same model, it is a better method. For multiple mediators, AMOS cannot directly estimate the statistical significance of specific indirect effects. Therefore, PRODCLIN, a program computing confidence limits for the product of two normal random variables, is also utilized by the researcher in this study. According to Mackinnon, Fritz, William and Lockwood (2007), PRODCLIN can be employed to obtain more accurate confidence limits for the indirect effects.

5.4.3 Practical Contribution

Apart from the theoretical and methodological contributions of this study, some practical contributions are also highlighted in this section.

The findings of this study can raise awareness among government, higher education management authorities and university management levels on the importance of identifying grassroots administrative staff in universities. This is because their work engagement and job performance which are found to be relatively low may specifically affect university administration level, the quality of higher education in general. In addition, their perception of organizational support is also not high, which shows that they are not valued by the organization. This result should probably be used as a reminder that in university management, attention should also be paid to the support for administrative staff when focusing on the academic and teaching staff. Finally, the study helps the higher education management community to recognize the seriousness of the problems of the administrative staff. It reveals that it is necessary to find effective ways to enhance the job performance of the administrative staff.

Practically, the results of this study have significant contributions to both higher education management and human resource management. It provides advantageous insights on how perceived organizational support and its dimensions can enhance job performance and its dimensions and how work engagement and its dimensions mediate the two variables. Thus, it helps in developing suitable improvement strategies for organization, especially for the newly-established university in China. For example, the study found that 76.4% of the variance of job performance is explained by the variables of perceiving organizational support and job performance. This shows that the two factors of organizational support and employee engagement must be taken into account when formulating management policies. The findings of analyzing mediation of work engagement also suggest that the positive effect of organizational support on job performance will be more powerful if enhancing work engagement is taken into consideration. Furthermore, the study suggests that the organization should first let employees feel that their value is recognized by the organization when considering the support for employees.

5.5 Suggestions and Implications in Management

In general, improving the job performance of grassroots administrative staff is basically related to the organizational support and work engagement in newly-established universities which are considered an important part of Chinese higher education system (Zhuang, 2016). According to the findings of this study, working support, identifying value and caring about well-being is significantly influencing job performance of administrative staff, and these influences are mediated by vigor, dedication and absorption fully or partially. Based on the research results, the following management suggestions are proposed for governments, higher education authorities, policymakers, and university leaders.

Firstly, to provide more material and spiritual support to administrative staff and let them feel this support from the university and society. This support includes working support, identifying value and caring about well-being (Ling et al., 2006). In terms of working support, it is considered to improve the office environment, equipped with the necessary office supplies, provide professional and effective job skills training, provide appropriate professional guidance, and develop rigorous, fair and positive incentives and management policies. In terms of identifying value, it is suggested to pay attention to the contribution of administrative staff, respect and recognize their value, give commendations and rewards to those with excellent grades, treat administrative staff and academic staff equally in management and provide opportunities for personal career development. Regarding caring about well-being, it can be considered giving reasonable and stimulating salaries and rewards, providing human welfare policies such as working meals and working shuttles, improving living and housing conditions, improving social security systems such as medical insurance and housing accumulation funds, formulating humanized working attendance systems and reasonable vacation system. On the three aspects of organizational support for administrative staff, value identification should be placed first. It must be made that the administrative staff feel that the organization attaches importance to them and fully recognizes their value.

Secondly, to create an engaged organizational culture, and establish a competitive organizational atmosphere and working atmosphere. According to the results of this study, work engagement should not only directly affect job performance, but should also play a mediator role, which is to help enhance the impact of perceived organizational support on job performance. Therefore, there is a need to create a good organizational culture and working atmosphere, establish a scientific and rational management system, and inspire administrative staff to be more engaged. Based on the three dimensions of work engagement which are vigor, dedication and absorption (Schaufeli et al., 2002), the following management recommendations are made: to establish a reasonable rank promotion mechanism and salary system to stimulate the vigor and absorption of administrative staff; to develop a competitive employment mechanism and a scientific assessment and evaluation system to force administrative staff to be more dedicated.

Thirdly, to change the job values of administrative staff. As this study concludes, the level of administrative staff' perception of identifying value by the organization is not high, which can be directly and indirectly reduce their job performance. In fact, some administrative staff feel that their achievements and contributions at work are hardly recognized by the leaders of the organization compared to academic staff. This kind of awareness negatively affects their work enthusiasm and passion. Therefore, it is necessary to change their opinion and find ways to make administrative staff realize that their value is recognized and identified by the organization. To be specific, it is important to strengthen the guidance of administrative staff on the job values through advocacy, training and learning to take into account the interests of administrative staff in the formulation of management policies, to improve incentive systems to reward employees who contribute to administrative work, and to emphasize the importance and value of administrative staff in university development planning.

Fourthly, to give administrative staff diverse humane cares. With the development of society and civilization, the use of economic means alone cannot solve the problems faced by the relationship between organizations and employees. The results of this study found that the organization's recognition of employees and the concern for employees has a significant effect on the employees' own engagement and involvement in the work, and thus affect the work performance of employees. Therefore, through the humanistic care of employees through ideas and behaviours, the organization can enhance employees' sense of belonging and loyalty to the organization, emotionally enhance employees' attachment to the organization, and thus encouraging more engagement in work to repay the organization and show a good job performance. Diversified humanistic care is an important form of enterprise-oriented human management. The university should also manage administrative staff in this way. For example, to occasionally organize administrative staff to carry out interesting activities or sports meetings so that they can get rid of boring from administrative work, to give spiritual and material assistance to administrative staff when they face with difficulties in their family or life. Through these measures, the administrative staff's sense of belonging to the university is strengthened, and the ownership spirit of the administrative staff is established, thereby improving the job performance of the administrative staff and the administrative level of the university. This will help achieve a win-win situation between the organization and the employees.

5.6 Future Research

Certainly, this study has provided evidence and support for the modeling relationship between perceived organizational support, work engagement and job performance of grassroots administrative staff in Chinese Newly-established universities. However, there are still some limitations which may guide future research.

It is suggested that more studies should be conducted on the relationship between perceived organizational support, work engagement and job performance among other industry practitioner groups or other demographic samples which may give rise to other significant findings. Similarly, for the generalization of the outcomes of this study, the present study should be replicated to involve other countries or other organizational backgrounds.

The quantitative research methodology is used in this study and self-determined questionnaire is adopted to collect data. Future research may adopt other research methods to expand the study scope and enrich the study findings, such as qualitative research and mixed research design. Even with quantitative research, other measurement scales can be developed to collect data which may lead to other valuable findings on different dimensions of perceived organizational support, work engagement and job performance.

As discussed earlier, Chinese newly-established universities face many challenges and suffer from many problems that have accumulated over several years. These problems are mainly financial, administrative and human resource deficits, as well as the imperfect management system. Therefore, in order to improve the quality of high education, further empirical research is needed to explore the factors influencing such situations.

5.7 Summary

Overall, this study is conducted to determine the modeling relationship between perceived organizational support, work engagement and job performance among administrative staff in Chinese newly-established universities. The study adopts a quantitative research method by using an online questionnaire to gather data from participants. In order to address the research questions and examine the hypotheses, SPSS and AMOS are utilized in the study. SPSS is used to conduct a preliminary data analysis such as detection of outliers, the test of normality, the test of common method variance, the test of non-response bias, descriptive analysis, examination of reliability and EFA. AMOS is used to build SEM for

CHAPTER FIVE: DISCUSSION AND CONCLUSION

confirmatory factor analysis and hypotheses test. The results reveal that there are positive relationships among perceived organizational support, work engagement and job performance. Besides, work engagement can mediate between perceiving organizational support and job performance.

By developing the research framework, building SEM and testing the relationship between perceived organizational support, work engagement and job performance, this research has added some contributions to both the academic and practical field. It also provides several implications for higher education authorities and newly established university management. Besides, it can serve as a theoretical background for further research in the field of higher education management or human resource management.

References

[1] ADAMS J S. Towards an understanding of inequity. The Journal of Abnormal and Social Psychology, 1963, 67(5), 422-436.

[2] AFZALI A, ARASH MOTAHARI A & HATAMI-SHIRKOUHI L. Investigating the influence of perceived organizational support, psychological empowerment and organizational learning on job performance: an empirical investigation. Tehnički vjesnik, 2014, 21(3), 623-629.

[3] AHMED S. Methods in sample surveys. Johns Hopkins Bloomberg School of Public, 2009.

[4] AKGUNDUZ Y & SANLI S C. The effect of employee advocacy and perceived organizational support on job embeddedness and turnover intention in hotels. Journal of Hospitality and Tourism Management, 2017, 31, 118-125.

[5] ALBRIGHT J J & PARK H M. Confirmatory factor analysis using Amos, LISREL, Mplus, SAS/STAT CALIS. University Information Technology Services Center for Statistical and Mathematical Computing, Indiana University, 2009.

[6] AL-DALAHMEH M, KHALAF R & OBEIDAT B. The effect of employee

engagement on organizational performance via the mediating role of job satisfaction: The case of IT employees in the Jordanian banking sector. Modern Applied Science, 2018, 12(6), 17-43.

[7] ALDERFER C P. An empirical test of a new theory of human needs. Organizational Behavior and Human Performance, 1969, 4(2), 142-175.

[8] ALDERFER C P. Existence, Relatedness, and Growth; Human Needs in Organizational Settings, New York: Free Press, 1972.

[9] ALDERFER C P, PORTER L W & LAWLER E E. Managerial attitudes and performance. Administrative Science Quarterly, 1968, 13(1), 177.

[10] ALESSANDRI G, BORGOGNI L & LATHAM G P. A dynamic model of the longitudinal relationship between job satisfaction and supervisor-rated job performance. Applied Psychology, 2017, 66(2), 207-232.

[11] ALFES K, SHANTZ A D, TRUSS C & SOANE E C. The link between perceived human resource management practices, engagement and employee behavior: a moderated mediation model. The International Journal of Human Resource Management, 2013, 24(2), 330-351.

[12] ALFES K, TRUSS C, SOANE E C, REES C & GATENBY M. The Relationship Between Line Manager Behavior, Perceived HRM Practices, and Individual Performance: Examining the Mediating Role of Engagement. Human Resource Management, 2013, 52(6), 839-859.

[13] ALLEN T D. Family-supportive work environments: The role of organizational

perceptions. Journal of vocational behavior, 2001, 58(3), 414-435.

[14] ANITHA J. Determinants of employee engagement and their impact on employee performance. International Journal of Productivity and Performance Management, 2014, 63(3), 308.

[15] ARGYRIS C. Understanding organizational behavior. Dorsey Press: Homewood, 1960.

[16] ARMELI S, EISENBERGER R, FASOLO P & LYNCH P. Perceived organizational support and police performance: The moderating influence of socioemotional needs. Journal of Applied Psychology, 1998, 83(2), 288-297.

[17] ARMSTRONG J S. Illusions in regression analysis. International Journal of Forecasting, 2012, 28(3), 689-694.

[18] ARMSTRONG J S & OVERTON T S. Estimating non response bias in mail surveys. Journal of marketing research, 1977, 14(3), 396-402

[19] ARMSTRONG R L. The midpoint on a five-point Likert-type scale. Perceptual and Motor Skills, 1987, 64(2), 359-362.

[20] AWANG Z. Structural equation modeling using AMOS graphic. Penerbit Universiti Teknologi MARA, 2012.

[21] BABBIE E. Practice of business and social research. Capetown: Oxford University Press, 2000.

[22] BAGOZZI R P, YI Y & PHILLIPS L W. Assessing construct validity in organizational research. Administrative Science Quarterly, 1991, 36 (3), 421-458.

[23] BAKKER A B & BAL M P. Weekly work engagement and performance: A study among starting teachers. Journal of Occupational and Organizational Psychology, 2010, 83(1), 189-206.

[24] BAKKER A B & DEMEROUTI E. Job demands–resources theory. Wellbeing: A complete reference guide, 2014, 1-28.

[25] BAKKER A & DEMEROUTI E. Job demands–resources theory: Taking stock and looking forward. Journal of Occupational Health Psychology, 2017, 22(3), 273-285.

[26] BAKKER A & SANZ-VERGEL A I. Weekly work engagement and flourishing: The role of hindrance and challenge job demands. Journal of Vocational Behavior, 2013, 83(3), 397-409.

[27] BAKKER A B, SANZ VERGEL A I & KUNTZE J. Student engagement and performance: A weekly diary study on the role of openness. motivation and emotion, 2014, 39(1), 49-62.

[28] BARKSDALE K & WERNER J M. Managerial ratings of in-role behaviors, organizational citizenship behaviors, and overall performance: testing different models of their relationship. Journal of Business Research, 2001, 51(2), 145-155.

[29] BARNARD C I. Organization and management. London: Routledge, 2003.

[30] BARON R M & KENNY D A. The moderator-mediator variable distinction in social psychological research: Conceptual, strategic, and statistical considerations. Journal of Personality and social Psychology, 1986, 51 (6), 1173-1182.

[31] BARTLETT II J E, KOTRLIK J W & HIGGINS C C. Organizational Research: Determining Appropriate Sample Size in Survey Research. Information Technology, Learning, And Performance Journal, 2001, 19(1), 43-50.

[32] BELL S J & MENGUC B. The employee-organization relationship, organizational citizenship behaviors, and superior service quality. Journal of Retailing, 2002, 78(2), 131-146.

[33] BENTLER P M. Comparative fit indexes in structural models. Psychological Bulletin, 1990, 107(2), 238-246.

[34] BERNARDIN H J & BEATTY R W. Performance appraisal. Boston, Mass.: Kent Publ. Co, 1984.

[35] BI Y, CAI Y H & CAI J. The Relationship among Pay Satisfaction, Perceived Organizational Support and Teacher Performance. Journal of Education Studies, 2016, 12(2), 81-88.

[36] BLAU P M. Justice in Social Exchange. Sociological Inquiry, 1964, 34(2), 193-206.

[37] BOLARINWA O. Principles and methods of validity and reliability testing of questionnaires used in social and health science researches. Nigerian Postgraduate Medical Journal, 2015, 22(4), 195.

[38] BORMAN W C & MOTOWIDLO S J. Expanding the criterion domain to include elements of contextual performance. Personnel Selection In Organizations, 1993, 71-98.

[39] BORMAN W C & MOTOWIDLO S M. Task Performance and Contextual Performance: The Meaning for Personnel Selection Research. Human Performance, 1997, 10(2), 99-109.

[40] BOURQUE L & FIELDER E P. How to conduct self-administered and mail surveys (Vol. 3). Sage, 2003.

[41] BRITT T W, ADLER A B & BARTONE P T. Deriving benefits from stressful events: The role of engagement in meaningful work and hardiness. Journal of Occupational Health Psychology, 2001, 6(1), 53-63.

[42] BROWN R L. Assessing specific mediational effects in complex theoretical models. Structural Equation Modeling, 1997, 4, 142-156

[43] BRUMBACK G B. Some Ideas, Issues and Predictions about Performance Management. Public Personnel Management, 1988, 17(4), 387-402.

[44] BUIL I, MARTÍNEZ E & MATUTE J. Transformational leadership and employee performance: The role of identification, engagement and proactive personality. International Journal of Hospitality Management, 2019, 77, 64-75.

[45] BURNS A C. & BUSH R F. Marketing research. Upper Saddle River, N.J: Pearson/Prentice Hall, 2005.

[46] BYARS L L & RUE L W. Human resource management. Boston: Irwin, 1994.

[47] BYRNE B. Structural equation modeling with AMOS basic concepts, applications and programming (2 ed). New York: Routledge Taylor & Francis Group, 2010.

[48] BYRNE M S. Factors involved in the learning of consumer studies. Journal of

Consumer Studies and Home Economics, 2001, 25(4), 322-330.

[49] CABLE D M & JUDGE T A. Pay Preferences and Job Search Decision: A Person-Organization Fit Perspective. Personnel Psychology, 1994, 47(2), 317-348.

[50] CAESENS G & STINGLHAMBER F. The relationship between perceived organizational support and work engagement: The role of self-efficacy and its outcomes. Revue Européenne De Psychologie Appliquée/European Review of Applied Psychology, 2014, 64(5), 259-267.

[51] CAI W. Research on the Influence of Workplace Friendship and Organizational Commitment on Employee's Performance (Unpublished master's thesis). Guangdong University of Finance and Economics, 2015.

[52] CAO W L, PENG C H & LIANG L. Research on job engagement and job burnout on abroad. Science Research Management, 2013, 34(12), 156-160.

[53] CAMPBELL J P, MCHENRY J J & WISE L L. Modeling Job Performance in a Population of Jobs. Personnel Psychology, 1990, 43(2), 313-575.

[54] CAMPBELL J P. Modeling the Performance Prediction Problem in Industrial and Organizational Psychology. Handbook of Industrial and Organizational Psychology, Palo Alto: Consulting Psychologists Press, 1990.

[55] CAMPBELL J P, MCCLOY R A, OPPLER S H & SAGER C E. A theory of performance. Personnel selection in organizations, 1993, 35-70.

[56] CAMPBELL J P. Improving the selection, classification, and utilization of Army enlisted personnel: Annual report, 1985 fiscal year. ARI Technical Report 746.

Arlington, VA: Army Research Institute for the Behavioral and Social Sciences, 1987.

[57] CAO K Y & NING W. Influence of Human Resource Management Practice of Employee Engagement: Empirical Research on Mediating Role of Perceived Organizational Support. Science and Technology Management Research, 2012, (5), 174-178.

[58] CATHCART D, JESKA S, KARNAS J. et al. Span of Control Matters. The Journal of Nursing Administration, 2004, 34(9), 395-399.

[59] CESÁRIO F & CHAMBEL M J. Linking organizational commitment and work engagement to employee performance. Knowledge and Process Management, 2017, 24(2), 152-158.

[60] CHA S C. The study on building the structure model of employee engagement in enterprises (Unpublished master's thesis). Jinan University, 2007.

[61] CHAUDHARY R & AKHOURI A. Linking corporate social responsibility attributions and creativity: Modeling work engagement as a mediator. Journal of Cleaner Production, 2018, 190, 809-821.

[62] CHEN J A & ZHANG J W. Promote employee engagement with a trust repair plan. Human Resource Development of China, 2010, (1), 26-29.

[63] CHEN L & DUAN X M. Literature review on the performance structure theory based on behavior. Science Research Management, 2008, 29(2), 133-142.

[64] CHEN L & DUAN X M. A Study of the Mid-level Supervisors' Performance

Evaluation Structure Based on Behavior. Journal of Industrial Engineering Engineering Management, 2009, 23(2), 44-49.

[65] CHEN R. A Study on the Job Satisfaction of Administrative Staff in Guangdong Colleges and Universities (Unpublished master's thesis). Sun Yat - sen University, 2017.

[66] CHEN S & YIN X F. An Empirical Study on the Relationship between Organizational Support and Job Performance in China's Real Estate Industry. Journal of Capital University of Economics and Business, 2009, (5), 69-74.

[67] CHEN X P, XU S Y & FAN J L. An Empirical Method of Organizational and Management Research (2nd ed.). Beijing: Peking University Press, 2012.

[68] CHEN Z X & CHEN J F. The Direct and Indirect Effects of Knowledge-worker's Perceived Organizational Support to Their Job Performance. Industrial Engineering and Management, 2008, 13(1), 99-104.

[69] CHIANG C F & HSIEH T S. The impacts of perceived organizational support and psychological empowerment on job performance: The mediating effects of organizational citizenship behavior. International journal of hospitality management, 2012, 31(1), 180-190.

[70] Chinese Education Ministry. Trial Measures for the Establishment of Ordinary Institutions of Higher Education. Beijing: Chinese Education Ministry, 1985.

[71] Chinese Education Ministry. Guidance on the implementation of post setting and management in Colleges and Universities. Beijing: Chinese Education

Ministry, 2007.

[72] Chinese National Development and Reform Commission. The development plan of Chengdu-Chongqing Economic Zone. Beijing: Chinese National Development and Reform Commission, 2011.

[73] Chinese National Human Resources Ministry. Opinions on the implementation of post setting and management in Institutional Organization. Beijing: Chinese National Human Resources Ministry, 2006.

[74] CHONG H, WHITE R E & PRYBUTOK V. Relationship among organizational support, JIT implementation, and performance. Industrial Management & Data Systems, 2001, 101(6), 273-281.

[75] COOPER C L & CLEGG S. The Sage handbook of organizational behavior. Sage, 2008.

[76] COOPER D & SCHINDLER P. Business Research Methods (12th Ed.). New York: McGrawHill, 2014.

[77] COUPER M P. Advantages and Disadvantages of Internet Survey Methods for Official Statistics. Daejeon: 4th International Workshop on Internet Survey Methods, 2012.

[78] CRESWELL J W. Research design. Thousand Oaks, Calif.: Sage Publications, 2003.

[79] CRESWELL J W & CLARK V L P. Designing and conducting mixed methods research. Thousand Oaks, Calif.: Sage Publications, 2007.

[80] CRESWELL J W & CRESWELL J W. Qualitative inquiry and research design. Los Angeles: Sage Publications, 2013.

[81] CRESWELL J, W & PLANO CLARK V L. Designing and conducting mixed methods research. Thousand Oaks: Sage, 2009.

[82] CROWNE D P & MARLOWE D. A new scale of social desirability independent of psychopathology. Journal of Consulting Psychology, 1960, 24(4), 349-354.

[83] CRONBACH L. Coefficient alpha and the internal structure of tests. Psychometrika, 1951, 16(3), 297-334.

[84] CUTTANCE P. Curriculum: the frog-prince of school effectiveness research?. Journal of Curriculum Studies, 1987, 19(1), 77-85.

[85] DARLING-HAMMOND L, WISE A E & PEASE S R. Teacher Evaluation in the Organizational Context: A Review of the Literature. Review of Educational Research, 1983, 53(3), 285-328.

[86] DECONINCK J & DECONINCK M B. The Relationship between Servant Leadership, Perceived Organizational Support, Performance, and Turnover among Business to Business Sales people. Archives of Business Research, 2017, 5(10).

[87] DECI E L.Intrinsic motivation. New York: Plenum P, 1975.

[88] DECI E L & RYAN R M. The empirical exploration of intrinsic motivational processes. Advances in Experimental Social Psychology, 1980, 13(08), 39-80.

[89] DECI E & RYAN R M. Intrinsic Motivation and Self-Determination in Human Behavior. New York: Plenum, 1985.

[90] DECI E L & RYAN R M. The what and why of goal pursuits: Human needs and the self-determination of behavior. Psychological inquiry, 2000, 11(4), 227-268.

[91] DEMEROUTI E, BAKKER A B, NACHREINER F & SCHAUFELI W B. The job demands-resources model of burnout. Journal of Applied psychology, 2001, 86 (3), 499-512.

[92] Dillman D A. Mail and internet surveys: The tailored design method. New York: Wiley, 2000.

[93] DING Y J. Research on the Incentive Mode of Grass - roots Administrative Staff in Colleges and Universities (Unpublished master's thesis). Guizhou University, 2009.

[94] DONG X L & MA L J. Relationship of competence and performance of the administrative staff in higher education institutions. Journal of Higher Education, 2013, 34(10), 22-27.

[95] DWIGHT S A & FEIGELSON M E. A quantitative review of the effect of computerized testing on the measurement of social desirability. Educational and psychological measurement, 2000, 60(3), 340-360.

[96] EDMONDSON D & BOYER S. The Moderating Effect of the Boundary Spanning Role on Perceived Supervisory Support: A Meta-Analytic Review. Journal of Business Research, 201366(11), 2186-2192.

[97] EISENBERGER R, ARMELI S, REXWINKEL B, LYNCH P D & RHOADES L. Reciprocation of perceived organizational support. Journal of Applied

Psychology, 2001, 86(1), 42-51.

[98] EISENBERGER R, HUNTINGTON R, HUTCHISON S & SOWA D. Perceived organizational support. Journal of Applied Psychology, 1986, 71(3), 500-507.

[99] EISENBERGER R, STINGLHAMBER F, VANDENBERGHE C, SUCHARSKI I & RHOADES L. Perceived supervisor support: Contributions to perceived organizational support and employee retention. Journal of Applied Psychology, 2002, 87(3), 565-573.

[100] ENNIS R H. Operational Definitions. American Educational Research Journal, 1964, 1(3), 183.

[101] EXTREMERA N, SÁNCHEZ-GARCÍA M, DURÁN M & REY L. Examining the Psychometric Properties of the Utrecht Work Engagement Scale in Two Spanish Multi-occupational Samples. International Journal of Selection and Assessment, 2012, 20(1), 105-110.

[102] FAN S P. The study of relationship among perceived organizational support, employee's engagement and job performance (Unpublished master's thesis). Southwestern University of Finance and Economics, 2012.

[103] FANG J, WEN Z L, ZHANG M Q & SUN P Z. The Analyses of Multiple Mediation Effects Based on Structural Equation Modeling. Journal of Psychological Science, 2014, 37(3), 735-741

[104] FANG G Z, SUN X M & YANG X. Design of the University Teacher's Comprehensive Performance Appraisal System. Journal of Northeast Normal

University (Philosophy and Social Sciences) 2006, (3), 156-160.

[105] FEMI A F. The impact of communication on workers' performance in selected organisations in Lagos State, Nigeria. IOSR Journal of Humanities and Social Science, 2014, 19(8), 75-82.

[106] FENG C L & YANG X Y. The Influence of Transaction Leadership on Task Performance: The Mediating Role of Work Engagement. Journal of Ludong University (Natural Science Edition), 2018, 34(2), 178-183

[107] FERNANDEZ S & PITTS D W. Understanding Employee Motivation to Innovate: Evidence from Front Line Employees in United States Federal Agencies. Australian Journal of Public Administration, 2011, 70(2), 202-222.

[108] FINCHAM J E. Response rates and responsiveness for surveys, standards, and the journal. American Journal of Pharmaceutical Education, 2008, 72(2), 43.

[109] FISKE S T & TAYLOR S E. Social cognition (2nd ed.). New York: McGraw-Hill, 1991.

[110] FORNELL C & LARCKER D F. Evaluating structural equation models with unobservable variables and measurement error. Journal of marketing research, 1981, 18(1), 39-50.

[111] FORZA C & FILIPPINI R. TQM impact on quality conformance and customer satisfaction: a causal model. International journal of production economics, 1998, 55(1), 1-20.

[112] FOWLER F J. Survey research methods. London: Sage Publication, 2014.

[113] GALLUP. The high cost of disengaged employees. Business Journal. Retrieved from:http://www.gallup.com/businessjournal/247/the-high-cost-ofdisengaged-employees.aspx, 2002.

[114] GAN Q Y. Thought of Evaluation on Teachers' Work in Colleges and Universities. Journal of Guizhou University for Ethnic Minorities (Philosophy And Social Science), 2006, (1), 148-151.

[115] GAO J. A Study on College Grass-root Administrators' Job Burnout - A Case Study of a Certain University in Changzhou (Unpublished Master's thesis). Soochow University, 2015.

[116] GAULT R H. A History of the Questionnaire Method of Research in Psychology. The Pedagogical Seminary, 1907, 14(3), 366-383.

[117] GEORGE D & MALLERY M. SPSS for Windows Step by Step: A Simple Guide and Reference, 17.0 update. Boston: Pearson, 2010.

[118] GEORGE J M & BRIEF A P. Feeling good-doing good: A conceptual analysis of the mood at work-organizational spontaneity relationship. Psychological Bulletin, 1992, 112(2), 310-329.

[119] GEORGE J M, REED T F, BALLARD K A, et al.Contact with Aids Patients as a Source of Work-related Distress: Effects of Organizational and Social Support. Academy Of Management Journal, 1993, 36(1), 157-171.

[120] GOULDNER A W.The Norm of Reciprocity: A Preliminary Statement. American Sociological Review, 1960, 25(2), 161.

[121] GRAHAM S AND FOLKES V S. Attribution theory. Hoboken: Psychology Press/Taylor & Francis Group, 2014.

[122] GREENSPOON P J & SAKLOFSKE D H. Confirmatory factor analysis of the multidimensional Student's Life Satisfaction Scale. Personality and Individual Differences, 1998, 25, 965-971.

[123] GROBELNA A. Effects of individual and job characteristics on hotel contact employees' work engagement and their performance outcomes: A case study from Poland. International Journal of Contemporary Hospitality Management, 2019, 31(1), 349-369.

[124] GU Y A. Thoughts and suggestions based on the analysis of setting in newly-built undergraduate colleges. China Higher Education Research, 2012, 28(2), 68-73.

[125] GUAN X & FRENKEL S. How HR practice, work engagement and job crafting influence employee performance. Chinese Management Studies, 2018, 12(3), 591-607.

[126] GUO Y X, DU H F, XIE B G & MO L Work engagement and job performance: the moderating role of perceived organizational support. Anales De Psicología, 2017, 33(3), 708.

[127] HAIR J F, ANDERSON R E, TATHAM R L. et al. *Multivariate data analysis*. (5th ed.). Prentice-Hall, New Jersey, 1998.

[128] Hair J F, Black W C, Babin B J. et al. *Multivariate data analysis*. Upper Saddle

River, N.J.: Pearson Prentice Hall, 2006.

[129] HAIR J F, BLACK B, BABIN B, et al. *Multivariate Data Analysis: A Global Perspective*. New Jersey, USA: Pearson Education Inc, 2010.

[130] HAIR J F, HULT G T M, RINGLE C & SARSTEDT M. A primer on partial least squares structural equation modeling (PLS-SEM). Washington DC: SAGE Publications, 2014.

[131] HALL D T & GOODALE J G. Human resource management. Glenview, Ill.: Scott, Foresman, 1986.

[132] HAN Y. A Casual Model of Development and Empirical Study on Employee Job Performance Construct (Unpublished doctoral thesis). Huazhong University of Science and Technology, 2006.

[133] HAN Y M. On Innovating Administrative System of Newly -Built Undergraduate Colleges. Research in Higher Education of Engineering, 2009, 27(4), 100-104.

[134] HAY GROUP. Employee Engagement: the Key to Realizing Competitive Advantage. Retrieved from http://www.ddiworld.com/DDIWorld/media/monographs/employeeengagement_mg_ddi.pdf?ext=.pdf, 2009.

[135] HAYTON J C, CARNABUCI G & EISENBERGER R. With a little help from my colleagues: A social embeddedness approach to perceived organizational support. Journal of organizational Behavior, 2011, 33(2), 235-249.

[136] HE T. The Discussion of Online Questionnaire. Computer Knowledge and Technology, 2016, 12(13), 32-36.

[137] HEIDER F. The Psychology of Interpersonal Relations. New York: Wiley, 1958.

[138] HENSON R K & ROBERTS J K. Use of Exploratory Factor Analysis in Published Research. Educational and Psychological Measurement, 2006, 66(3), 393-416.

[139] HENSON R K & ROBERTS J K. Use of Exploratory Factor Analysis in Published Research. Educational and Psychological Measurement, 2006, 66(3), 393-416.

[140] HEWITT ASSOCIATES Hewitt Associates study shows more engaged employees drive improved business performance and return. Retrieved from https://www.businesswire.com/news/home/20040518005156/en/Hewitt-Associates-Study-Shows-Engaged-Employees-Drive, 2004.

[141] HEWSTONE M & JASPARS J. Covariation and causal attribution: A Logical Model of the intuitive analysis of variance. Journal of Personality And Social Psychology, 1987, 53(4), 663-672.

[142] Higher Education Evaluation Center of the Chinese Ministry of Education. (2018). Chinese Higher Education Quality Report. Beijing.

[143] HINKLE D E & OLIVER J D. How large should the sample be? A question with no simple answer? Educational and Psychological Measurement, 1983, 43(4), 1051-1060.

[144] HOLBERT R L & STEPHENSON M T. The importance of Indirect Effects in Media Effects Research: Testing for mediation in Structural Modeling. Journal of

Broadcasting & Electronic Media, 2003, 47(4), 556-572.

[145] HOLLAND P, COOPER B & SHEEHAN C. Employee Voice, Supervisor Support, and Engagement: The Mediating Role of Trust. Human Resource Management, 2016, 56(6), 915-929.

[146] HOMANS G C. Social Behavior as Exchange. American Journal of Sociology, 1958, 63(6), 597-606.

[147] HOU L Y & CHEN B Y. Individual Differences, Sense of Organization Aid and Work Achievements. Journal of Shenzhen University (Humanities & Social Sciences), 2011, 28(2), 74-78.

[148] HU D. A study on the relationship between job stress and self-efficacy on work performance (Unpublished master's thesis). Hangzhou Dianzi University, 2009.

[149] HU S N & WANG Y. Concept, Measurement, Antecedents and Consequences of Work Engagement. Advances in Psychological Science, 2014, 22(12), 1975-1984.

[150] HU W F & LIU H L. An Empirical Study of the Perceived Organizational Support and Work Engagement of Junior Middle School Teachers. JiangSu Education, 2016, (65), 27-33.

[151] HUO Y Y. A Study on the Dimension of Employee Engagement and Its Influencing Factors (Unpublished master's thesis). Zhejiang University, 2008.

[152] HUY Q N. Emotional Capability, Emotional Intelligence, and Radical Change. The Academy of Management Review, 1999, 24(2), 325.

[153] ISAAC S & MICHAEL W B. Handbook on research and evaluation. San Diego,

CA: EDITS Publishers, 1981.

[154] ISMAIL H, IQBAL A & NASR L. Employee engagement and job performance in Lebanon: the mediating role of creativity. International Journal of Productivity And Performance Management, 2019, 68(3), 506-523.

[155] JIAN H, WANG Z & TONG Z. Literature Review of Perceived Organizational Support. Destech Transactions on Social Science, Education and Human Science, (mess), 2017.

[156] JING R T, GAO X & LIU Y J. Review on Questionnaire survey in China: Situation and Suggestion. Management Scientist, 2008, (1), 53-57.

[157] JOHNSON S. Research, Research Everywhere: And Finally a Blog to Read! A Review of Nancy Walton's The Research Ethics Blog. AJOB Primary Research, 2010, 1(1), 46-47.

[158] JONES E E & DAVIS K E. From acts to dispositions: the attribution process in person perception. Advances in Experimental Social Psychology, 1965, (2), 219-266.

[159] JOY M W, KRISHNAN R. High Performance Work Systems – Implications for Perceived Organizational Support of Employees in Information Technology Sector. International Conference on Recent innovations in Sciences, Management, Education and Technology. Sirsa, Haryana, 2016.

[160] KAHN W A. Psychological Conditions of Personal Engagement and Disengagement at Work. Academy of Management Journal, 1990, 33(4), 692-724.

[161] KAHN W A .To Be Fully There: Psychological Presence at Work. Human Relations, 1992, 45(4), 321-349.

[162] KARATEPE O M & AGA M. The effects of organization mission fulfillment and perceived organizational support on job performance: The mediating role of work engagement. International Journal of Bank Marketing. 2016, 34(3), 368-387

[163] KAUFMAN J, STAMPER C & TESLUK P E. Do Supportive Organizations Make For Good Corporate Citizens. Journal Of Managerial Issues, 2001, 13(4), 436-449.

[164] KELLEY H H. Attribution theory in social psychology. Nebraska Symposium on Motivation, 1967, (15), 192-238.

[165] KELLEY H H. The process of causal attribution. American Psychologist, 1973, 28, 107-128.

[166] KERRY S & BLAND J. Statistics notes: Sample size in cluster randomisation. BMJ, 1998, 316(7130), 549-549.

[167] KIM H R. Managerial cognition, strategic behavior and innovation: Biopharmaceutical R & D. Pharmacy & Pharmacology International Journal, 2015, 2(1), 1-12

[168] KIM K Y, EISENBERGER R & BAIK K. Perceived Organizational Support and Organization Performance: HR, CEO, and Industry Influences. Academy Of Management Proceedings, 2017, (1), 14979.

[169] Kline R B. Principles and Practice of Structural Equation Modeling. New York:

The Guilford Press, 1998.

[170] KOTTER J P. The Psychological Contract: Managing the Joining-up Process. California Management Review, 1973, 15(3), 91-99.

[171] KO M S, LEE H Z & KOH M S. Effects of nurses' social capital and job engagement on nursing performance: Focused on the mediating effects of organizational citizenship behavior. Journal of Korean Academy of Nursing Administration, 2017, 23(1), 42.

[172] KRAIMER M L & WAYNE S J. An examination of perceived organizational support as a multidimensional construct in the context of an expatriate assignment. Journal of Management, 2004, 30(2), 209-237.

[173] KREJCIE R V & MORGAN D W. Determining sample size for research activities. Educational and Psychological Measurement, 1970, 30(3), 607-610.

[174] KURTESSIS J N, EISENBERGER R, FORD M T, et al. Perceived organizational support: A meta-analytic evaluation of organizational support theory. Journal of Management, 2017, 43(6), 1854-1884.

[175] LAHAUT V M, JANSEN H A, VAN DE MHEEN D & GARRETSEN H F. Non-response bias in a sample survey on alcohol consumption. Alcohol and Alcoholism, 2002, 37(3), 256-260.

[176] Lance P & A Hattori. Sampling and evaluation: A guide to sampling for program impact evaluation. Chapel Hill, North Carolina: University of North Carolina, 2016.

[177] LABRAGUE L J, MCENROE PETITTE D M, LEOCADIO M C. et al. Perceptions of organizational support and its impact on nurses' job outcomes. In Nursing forum, 2018.

[178] LEITER M P & SPENCE LASCHINGER H K. Relationships of Work and Practice Environment to Professional Burnout. Nursing Research, 2006, 55(2), 137-146.

[179] LEVINSON H. Reciprocation: the relationship between man and organization. Administrative Science Quarterly, 1965, 9(4), 370.

[180] LI R & LING W. A review of the research on work/job engagement. Advances In Psychological Science, 2007, 12(2), 366-372.

[181] LINDELL M K & WHITNEY D J. Accounting for common method variance in cross-selectional research designs. Journal of Applied Psychology, 2001, 86, 114-120.

[182] LING W Q, YANG H J & FANG L L. Perceived organizational support (POS) of the employees. Journal of Psychological Science, 2006, 38(2), 281-287.

[183] LIU H, CHEN M Q & CHEN M X. An empirical study on the effects of social identity and perceived organizational support on job involvement. Economic Forum, 2019, (582), 85-90.

[184] LIU J, YANG Y J, CHU H Y & ZHANG Y X. The mediating effect of nurses' psychological capital on organizational support and work engagement. Chinese Journal of Public Health, 2019.

[185] LIU K K. The comment on the statistics striding development of the newly-established undergraduate college. Journal of Taishan University, 2003, 25(1), 108-113.

[186] LIU L. A Study on the Relationship between Leadership Style, Psychological Contract and Employee Performance (Unpublished master's thesis). Nanjing University of Science and Technology, 2007.

[187] LIU Q Z. Research on the effect of university perceived organizational support on faculty performance (Unpublished master's thesis). Dalian University of Technology, 2015.

[188] LIU Q Z. & LI C. A Review of Researches on Organizational Support. In Establishment of scientific decision - making mechanism theory seminar (pp. 87-88). Wuhan: Institute of Higher Education, Dalian University of Technology, 2015.

[189] LIU S D & LING W Q. Multiple mediation models and their applications. Psychological Science, 2009, 32(2), 433-435.

[190] LUO A N. Research on the Relationship between Perceived Organizational Support, Engagement and Performance of High-level Talents in Research-intensive Universities (Unpublished doctoral thesis). Wuhan University, 2014.

[191] MA R J, WANG R K & ZUO X M. Principles of management. Beijing: Post & Telecom Press, 2013.

[192] MA W K. Research on the relationship between perceived organizational

support, job satisfaction and job performance - taking knowledge workers of new generation as an example (Unpublished master's thesis). East China Jiaotong University, 2016.

[193] MACEY W H & SCHNEIDER B. The meaning of employee engagement. Industrial and organizational Psychology, 2008, 1(1), 3-30.

[194] MACEY W H, SCHNEIDER B, BARBERA K M & YOUNG S A. Employee Engagement. New York, NY: John Wiley & Sons, 2011.

[195] MACKINNON D P. Introduction to Statistical Mediation Analysis. Mahwah, NJ: Earlbaum, 2008.

[196] MACKINNON D P, FRITZ M S, WILLIAM J & LOCKWOOD C M. Distribution of the product confidence limits for the indirect effect: Program PRODCLIN. Behavior Research Methods, 2007, 39(3), 384-389.

[197] MACKINNON D P, LOCKWOOD C M, HOFFMAN J M, et al. A comparison of methods to test mediation and other intervening variable effects. Psychological Methods, 2002, 7(1), 83-104.

[198] MACKINNON D P, LOCKWOOD C M & WILLIAMS J. Confidence limits for the indirect effect: Distribution of the product and resampling methods. Multivariate Behavioral Research, 2004, 39(1), 99-128.

[199] MÄKIKANGAS A, AUNOLA K, SEPPÄLÄ P & HAKANEN J. Work engagement-team performance relationship: shared job crafting as a moderator. Journal of Occupational and Organizational Psychology, 2016, 89(4), 772-790.

[200] MALHOTRA N K, DECAUDIN J & BOUGUERRA A. Études marketing avec SPSS. Paris: Pearson Education France, 2004.

[201] MALHOTRA N K, HALL J, SHAW M & OPPENHEIM P. Marketing research: An applied orientation (3th ed.) Frenchs Forest: Prentice Hall, 2006 .

[202] MARINGE F & MOURAD M. Marketing for Higher Education in Developing Countries: emphases and omissions. Journal of Marketing for Higher Education, 2012, 22(1), 1-9.

[203] MARSH H W & HOCEVAR D. The factorial invariance of student evaluations of college teaching. American Educational Research Journal, 1984, 21(2), 341-366.

[204] MASLACH C & LEITER M P. The truth about burnout: How organizations cause personal stress and what to do about it. San Francisco: Jossey-Bass, 1997.

[205] Maslach C & Leiter M P. The Truth about Burnout. Hoboken: John Wiley & Sons, 2008.

[206] MASLACH C, SCHAUFELI W B & LEITER M P. Job Burnout. Annual Review of Psychology, 2001, 52(1), 397-422.

[207] MASLOW A H. A theory of human motivation. Psychological Review, 1943, 50(4), 370-396.

[208] MAY D, GILSON R L & HARTER L M. The psychological conditions of meaningfulness, safety and availability and the engagement of the human spirit at work. Journal of Occupational and Organizational Psychology, 2004, 77(1), 11-37.

[209] MCKAY R B, BRESLOW M J, SANGSTER R L, et al. Translating survey

questionnaires: Lessons learned. New Directions for Evaluation, 1996(70), 93-104.

[210] MCMILLAN R. Customer satisfaction and organizational support for service providers. University of Florida, 1997.

[211] MEADOWS K A. So you want to do research? 5: Questionnaire design. *British Journal of Community Nursing*, 2003, 8(12), 562-570.

[212] MEINTJES A & HOFMEYR K. The impact of resilience and perceived organisational support on employee engagement in a competitive sales environment. SA Journal of Human Resource Management, 2018, 16(11), 1-11.

[213] MEMON M A, SALLEH R, NORDIN S M, et al. Person-organisation fit and turnover intention: The mediating role of work engagement. Journal of Management Development, 2018, 37(3), 285-298.

[214] MENGUC B, AUH S, FISHER M & HADDAD A. To be engaged or not to be engaged: The antecedents and consequences of service employee engagement. Journal of Business Research, 2013, 66(11), 2163-2170.

[215] MILLS M J, CULBERTSON S S & FULLAGAR C J. Conceptualizing and Measuring Engagement: An Analysis of the Utrecht Work Engagement Scale. Journal of Happiness Studies, 2011, 13(3), 519-545.

[216] MOHAMED A & ALI M. The influence of perceived organizational support on employees' job performance. International Journal of Scientific and Research Publications, 2015, 5(4), 1-6.

[217] MOOI E & SARSTEDT M. A concise guide to market research: The process, data, and methods using IBM SPSS statistics, Berlin: Springer Science & Business Media, 2011.

[218] MORTON S M, BANDARA D K, ROBINSON E M & CARR P E A. In the 21st Century, what is an acceptable response rate? Australian and New Zealand Journal of Public Health, 2012, 36(2), 106-108.

[219] MOTOWIDLO S J & VAN SCOTTER J R. Evidence that task performance should be distinguished from contextual performance. Journal of Applied Psychology, 1994, 79(4), 475-480.

[220] MULLER K E & PASOUR V B. Bias in linear model power and sample size due to estimating variance. Communications in Statistics - Theory and Methods, 1997, 26(4), 839-851.

[221] MURTHY R K. Perceived organizational support and work engagement. International Journal of Applied Research 2017, 3(5): 738-740.

[222] NEIL S T, KILBRIDE M, PITT L, et al. The questionnaire about the process of recovery (QPR): a measurement tool developed in collaboration with service users. Psychosis, 2009, 1(2), 145-155.

[223] NULTY D D. The adequacy of response rates to online and paper surveys: what can be done? Assessment & Evaluation in Higher Education, 2008, 33(3), 301-314.

[224] O'CATHAIN A & THOMAS K J. "Any other comments?" Open questions

on questionnaires – a bane or a bonus to research? BMC Medical Research Methodology, 2004, 4(1).

[225] O'DRISCOLL M P & RANDALL D M. Perceived Organisational Support, Satisfaction with Rewards, and Employee Job Involvement and Organisational Commitment. Applied Psychology, 1999, 48(2), 197-209.

[226] ORGAN D W. Organizational citizenship behavior: The good soldier syndrome. Lexington Books/DC Heath and Com, 1988.

[227] OWENS B P, BAKER W E, SUMPTER D M & CAMERON K S. Relational energy at work: Implications for job engagement and job performance. Journal of Applied Psychology, 2016, 101(1), 35-46.

[228] ÖZÇELİK G & UYARGİL C B. Performance Management Systems: Task-Contextual Dilemma Owing to the Involvement of the Psychological Contract and Organizational Citizenship Behavior. European Management Review, 2019, 16(2), 347-362.

[229] PALLANT J. SPSS survival manual: a step by step guide to data analysis using SPSS for window (2nd ed). Maidenhead: Open University Press, 2005.

[230] PARK H M. A one-way ANOVA allows to test whether several means (for different conditions or groups) are equal across one variable. The Trustees of Indiana University, 2003.

[231] PAULHUS D L. Measurement and control of response bias. In J. P. Robinson, P. R. Shaver, & L. S. Wrightsman (Eds.), Measures of social psychological attitudes,

Vol. 1. Measures of personality and social psychological attitudes (pp. 17-59). San Diego, CA, US: Academic Press, 1991.

[232] PEARCE C L & HERBIK P A. Citizenship Behavior at the Team Level of Analysis: The Effects of Team Leadership, Team Commitment, Perceived Team Support, and Team Size. The Journal of Social Psychology, 2004, 144(3), 293-310.

[233] PENG W & SAIDIN K. A Study of Relationship between Perceived Organizational Support and Work Engagement of Administrative Staff in Newly-Established Universities of China. Journal of Social Science Research, 2018, 12(2), 2756-2763.

[234] PENG Y. A Study on the Relationship between the Working Values and Engagement of Grass - roots Administrative Staff in Colleges and Universities. College Management, 2016, 11(5), 164.

[235] PENG Y & ZHANG H. On the Present Situation and Countermeasures of the Executives' Performance in Colleges and Universities. Journal of Taiyuan Urban Vocational College, 2016, (4), 167-168.

[236] PODSAKOFF P M, MACKENZIE S B & PODSAKOFF N P. Sources of method bias in social science research and recommendations on how to control it. Annual Review of Psychology, 2012, 63, 539-569.

[237] POURBARKHORDARI A, ZHOU E & POURKARIMI J. How Individual-focused Transformational Leadership Enhances Its Influence on Job Performance

through Employee Work Engagement. International Journal of Business And Management, 2016, 11(2), 249-261.

[238] PREACHER K J & HAYES A F. Asymptotic and resampling strategies for assessing and comparing indirect effects in multiple mediator models. Behavior Research Methods, 2008, 40(3), 879-891.

[239] QIN Y J. Research on the Relationship between Organizational Support and Job Performance of Knowledge Workers (Unpublished master's thesis). Southwestern University of Finance and Economics, 2009.

[240] QIU X M, ZHANG J & LIU X Q. Discussion on Strengthening the Ability of Local Economic Development in Newly Established Undergraduate Colleges. Economist, 2016, 333(11), 212-214.

[241] QU L P. A Study on the Relationship between Organizational Support Perception, Work Attitude and Work Results Based on Organizational Treatment (Unpublished master's thesis). Zhejiang University, 2006.

[242] RAFAELI A & WORLINE M. Individual emotion in work organizations. Social Science Information, 2001, 40(1), 95-123.

[243] RANDALL E SCHUMACKER & RICHARD G LOMAX. A Beginner's Guide to Structural Equation Modeling. New Jersey: Lawrence Erlbaum Associates, Publishers, 1996.

[244] RHOADES L & EISENBERGER R. Perceived organizational support: A review of the literature. Journal of Applied Psychology, 2002, 87(4), 698-714.

[245] RICH B L. Job engagement: Construct validation and relationships with job satisfaction, job involvement, and intrinsic motivation (Unpublished Doctoral thesis). University of Florida, 2006.

[246] RICH B L, LEPINE J A & CRAWFORD E R. Job Engagement: Antecedents and Effects on Job Performance. Academy of Management Journal, 2010, 53(3), 617-635.

[247] RICHARDSON F W. Enhancing Strategies to Improve Workplace Performance (Unpublished doctoral thesis). Walden University, 2014.

[248] RIGGLE R J, EDMONDSON D R & HANSEN J D. A meta-analysis of the relationship between perceived organizational support and job outcomes: 20 years of research. Journal of Business Research, 2009, 62(10), 1027-1030.

[249] ROBINSON D, PERRYMAN S & HAYDAY S. The Drivers of Employee Engagement. Brighton: Institute for Employment Studies, 2004.

[250] ROFCANIN Y, LAS HERAS M & BAKKER A B. Family supportive supervisor behaviors and organizational culture: Effects on work engagement and performance. Journal of Occupational Health Psychology, 2017, 22(2), 207-217.

[251] ROTHBARD N P. Enriching or Depleting? The Dynamics of Engagement in Work and Family Roles. Administrative Science Quarterly, 2001, 46(4), 655.

[252] ROTHMANN S & JOUBERT J H M. Job demands, job resources, burnout and work engagement of managers at a platinum mine in the North West Province. South African Journal of Business Management, 2007, 38(3), 49-61.

[253] ROTUNDO M & SACKETT P R. The relative importance of task, citizenship,

and counterproductive performance to global ratings of job performance: A policy-capturing approach. Journal of Applied Psychology, 2002, 87(1), 66-80.

[254] ROUSSEAU D M. Psychological contracts in organizations. Thousand Oaks: SAGE Publications, 1995.

[255] SAKS A M. Antecedents and consequences of employee engagement. Journal of Managerial Psychology, 2006, 21(7), 600-619.

[256] SALANOVA M, AGUT S & PEIRÓ J M. Linking Organizational Resources and Work Engagement to Employee Performance and Customer Loyalty: The Mediation of Service Climate. Journal of Applied Psychology, 2005, 90(6), 1217-1227.

[257] SAUNDERS M N K, LEWIS P & THORNHILL A. Research methods for business students. Harlow: FT-Prentice Hall, 2009.

[258] SCHAUFELI W B. What is engagement? In Employee engagement in theory and practice. London: Routledge, 2013.

[259] SCHAUFELI W B & BAKKER A B. Job demands, job resources, and their relationship with burnout and engagement: a multi-sample study. Journal of Organizational Behavior, 2004, 25(3), 293-315.

[260] SCHAUFELI W B, BAKKER A B & SALANOVA M. The Measurement of Work Engagement with a Short Questionnaire. Educational and Psychological Measurement, 2006, 66(4), 701-716.

[261] SCHAUFELI W B, BAKKER A B & VAN RHENEN W. How changes in job demands and resources predict burnout, work engagement, and sickness

absenteeism. Journal of Organizational Behavior, 2009, 30(7), 893-917.

[262] SCHAUFELI W B, SALANOVA M, GONZALEZ-ROMA V & BAKKER A B. The measurement of engagement and burnout: A confirmative analytic approach. Journal of Happiness Studies, 2002, 3, 71-92.

[263] SCHAUFELI W B, TARIS T W & VAN RHENEN W. Workaholism, Burnout, and Work Engagement: Three of a Kind or Three Different Kinds of Employee Well-being? Applied Psychology, 2008, 57(2), 173-203.

[264] SCHAUFELI W B & TARIS T W. A critical review of the job demands-resources model: Implications for improving work and health. In Bridging occupational, organizational and public health (pp. 43-68). Springer, Dordrecht, 2014.

[265] SCHAUFELI W B.The measurement of engagement and burnout: A two sample confirmatory factor analytic approach. Journal of Happiness Studies, 2002, (3), 71-92.

[266] SCHEIN E H & SCHEIN P. Organizational culture and leadership. San Francisco: Jossey-Bass Publishers, 1992.

[267] SCHULTZ D P & SCHULTZ S E. Psychology and Work Today: An Introduction to Industrial and Organizational Psychology (10th ed.). New York: Prentice Hall, 2010.

[268] SCHUMACKER R LOMAX R. A Beginner's Guide to Structural Equation Modeling (2nd Ed). Mahwah, NJ: Lawrence Erlbaum, 2004.

[269] SCHMITT N & BORMAN W C. Personnel selection in organizations. San

Francisco: Jossey-Bass, 1993.

[270] SEKARAN U U. Research Methods for business (4th ed.). John Wiley and Sons, 2003.

[271] SEKARAN U & BOUGIE R. Research methods for business. Chichester, West Sussex, United Kingdom: John Wiley & Sons, 2016.

[272] SEKARAN U & BOUGIE R. Research methods for business. (5th ed.). West Sussex UK: John Wiley & Sons, Inc, 2009.

[273] SHAO J. Employee Engagement and Manager Management Performance. China Collective Economy, 2007, (35).

[274] SHARMA J & DHAR R L. Factors influencing job performance of nursing staff: Mediating role of affective commitment. Personnel Review, 2016, 45(1), 161-182.

[275] SHI W. Genre of Attribution Theory and Related Research. Consume Guide, 2009, (10), 159.

[276] SHORE L M & TETRICK L E. A construct validity study of the Survey of Perceived Organizational Support. Journal of Applied Psychology, 1991, 76(5), 637-643.

[277] SHORE L M & WAYNE S J. Commitment and employee behavior: Comparison of affective commitment and continuance commitment with perceived organizational support. Journal of Applied Psychology, 1993, 78(5), 774-780.

[278] SHUCK B & WOLLARD K. Employee Engagement and HRD: A Seminal Review of the Foundations. Human Resource Development Review,

2009, 9(1), 89-110.

[279] SI Y Q. A Study on the Factors Affecting the Initiative of Grass-roots Administrative Staff in Colleges and Universities (Unpublished master's thesis). Northwest University, 2010.

[280] Sichuan Provincial Government. The Implementation Opinions on the Post Setting Management of Institutions in Sichuan Province. Chengdu: Sichuan Provincial Government, 2008.

[281] Sichuan Provincial Department of Education. The 13th Five-Year Plan for educational development of Sichuan Province (From 2016 to 2020). Chengdu: Sichuan Provincial Department of Education, 2017.

[282] SUN W M & LV C. Research on the relationship between POS and employees' engagement. Journal of Beijing Institute of Technology (Social Sciences Edition), 2012, 14(8), 67-73.

[283] TABACHNICK B & FIDELL L. Multivariate analysis of variance and covariance. Using Multivariate Statistics, 2007, 3, 402-407.

[284] TABACHNICK B G, FIDELL L S & ULLMAN J B. Using multivariate statistics (Vol. 5). Boston, MA: Pearson, 2007.

[285] TANG Y. Impact on employee engagement of organizational value and P-O value fit - a case study of R group (Unpublished master's thesis). Shandong Universtiy, 2009.

[286] GALLUP Employee Engagement: The Employee side of the Human Sigma

Equation. Retrieved from http://www.gallup.com/content/default.aspx?ci=52, 2005.

[287] TOWERS PERRIN Working today: Understanding what drives employee engagement. Retrieved from www.towersperrin.com/hrservices/webcache/ towers/ United_States/publications/Reports/Talent_Report_2003/Talent_2003.pdf, 2003.

[288] VAN SCOTTER J R & MOTOWIDLO S J. Interpersonal facilitation and job dedication as separate facets of contextual performance. Journal of Applied Psychology, 1996, 81(5), 525-531.

[289] VROOM V H. Work and motivation. San Francisco: Jossey-Bass, 1964.

[290] WANG B. Research on the regional economic development of Newly - established undergraduate colleges and universities in Sichuan. Co-Operative Economy & Science, 2016, 32(7), 76-77.

[291] WANG H F. Research on employee total rewards perceptions, engagement and job performance of non-state-owned enterprises (Unpublished doctoral thesis). Shanxi University of Finance & Economics, 2015.

[292] WANG H F & YANG J Q. The Effect of Employee Total Rewards and Demands-abilities Fit on Job Satisfaction: Taking Non-state-owned Enterprises for Example. On Economic Problems, 2015, (5), 73-78.

[293] WANG H, LI X X & LUO S Q. The Distinction of Task Performance and Contextual Performance and Their Effects on Work Outcomes. Chinese Journal of Management Science, 2003, 11(4), 79-84.

[294] WANG J W & DUAN Y S. China 's fourth largest economic growth pole - Chengdu - Chongqing Economic Zone. Education of Geography, 2011, 32(12), 57-58.

[295] WANG M F. Research on the Relationship between Knowledge - based Employee 's Vocation Orientation, Employee Engagement and Job Performance (Unpublished doctoral thesis). Capital University of Economics and Business, 2014.

[296] WANG W W. Study on the relationship of employees' perceived organizational support, psychological ownership and voice behavior (Unpublished doctoral thesis). Jilin University, 2014.

[297] WANG X X, LIU L, ZOU F T, et al. Associations of Occupational Stressors, Perceived Organizational Support, and Psychological Capital with Work Engagement among Chinese Female Nurses. Biomed Research International, 2017, 1-11.

[298] WEIERS R M. Introductory business statistics. Mason, Ohio: South-Western, 2011.

[299] WATSON D, CLARK L & TELLEGEN A. Development and validation of brief measures of positive and negative affect: The PANAS scales. Journal of Personality and Social Psychology, 1988, 54(6), 1063-1070.

[300] WEN B Y, ZHOU X M & WU X M. An Empirical Study of the Relationship among Positive Psychological Capital, Work Engagement and Job Performance in

Service Industry. Economic Survey, 2017, 34(3), 93-98.

[301] WICKRAMASINGHE N D, DISSANAYAKE D S & ABEYWARDENA G S. Validity and reliability of the Utrecht Work Engagement Scale-Student Version in Sri Lanka. BMC Research Notes, 2018, 11(1).

[302] WILLIAMS C. Research Methods. Journal of Business & Economics Research (JBER), 2011, 5(3).

[303] WILLIAMS F & MONGE P R. Reasoning with statistics. Fort Worth (TX): Harcourt College Publ, 2001.

[304] WRIGHT C, CARLING C, LAWLOR C AND COLLINS D. Elite football player engagement with performance analysis. International Journal of Performance Analysis in Sport, 2016, 16(3), 1007-1032.

[305] Wu M L. SPSS operation and application: The practice of quantitative analysis of questionnaire data. Taipei: Wu-Nan Book Co., Ltd, 2009.

[306] XANTHOPOULOU D, BAKKER A B, DEMEROUTI E & SCHAUFELI W B. Work Engagement and Financial Returns: A Diary Study on the Role of Job and Personal Resources. Journal of Occupational and Organizational Psychology, 2009, 82(1), 183-200.

[307] XIA L P. A Study on the Relationship between Emotional Characteristics, Working Family Relationship and Job Performance of Bankers (Unpublished master's thesis). Hunan Normal University, 2010.

[308] Xu W H. Research on survival state of basic level administrative staff - Based

on a survey in a college (Unpublished master's thesis). East China Normal University, 2007.

[309] XU X F, CHE H S, LIN X H & ZHANG J M. About the Organizational Support Theory. Psychological Science, 2005, 42(01), 130-132.

[310] YANG B. A Study on the Promotion of Employee Engagement in Chinese Enterprises: A Perspective of Organizational Atmosphere. Beijing: Capital University of Economics and Business Press, 2012.

[311] Yang H J. A Study on the Relationship between Competence and Performance of Administrative Staff in Colleges and Universities. Ability and Wisdom, 2017, 17(20), 122-123.

[312] YANG H M & LIAO J Q. An Analysis of the Status Quo of Employee Engagement and Its Future. Foreign Economics &Management, 2009, 31(5), 45-59.

[313] YANG X G. Pragmatic Research on work Engagement of Primary and Secondary School Teachers (Unpublished doctoral thesis). Southwestern University of Finance and Economics, 2008.

[314] YANG Y M. Discussion on the innovation of administrative work in colleges and universities. The Science Education Article Collects, 2007, 4(2), 128-129.

[315] YU D C. The Effect of Quality Factors on Performance of Quality Managers (Unpublished doctoral thesis). National Sun Yat - sen University, 1996.

[316] YU H Y & ZHU J. A Study on the Public Service Motivation of the Communist Youth League Cadres - Taking the Specialized Cadres in Beijing as an Example.

Journal of China Youth University for Political Sciences, 2014, (4).

[317] YU L Z, LIU F J & LIU D H. The construction of HRM faculty-based specialty orientation. Higher Education Forum, 2013, 29(8), 97-104.

[318] ZAINUDIN A. A Handbook on SEM for academicians and practitioners. The step by step practical guides for the beginners. Malaysia: MPWS Rich Resources, 2014.

[319] ZAIT A & BERTEA P. xMethods for testing discriminant validity. Management & Marketing, 2014, 9 (2), 217-224

[320] ZENG H & HAN J L. Improve employee engagement. Enterprise Management, 2005, (5), 99-101.

[321] ZHANG A Q. The research on job burnout and incentive strategy of grass-roots administrators of colleges and universities (Unpublished master's thesis). Northwest University, 2016.

[322] ZHANG D P. Research on the Relationship between Psychological Capital, Engagement and Job Performance of Small and Medium - sized Employees (Unpublished master's thesis). Ludong university, 2016.

[323] ZHANG J, ZHANG W & SONG Y H. Creation and Prosperity: Development of Self-determination Theory. Journal of University of Science and Technology Beijing (Social Sciences Edition), 2011, 27(4), 131-137.

[324] ZHANG S L. A review about perceived organizational support research. Science of Social Psychology, 2011, 26(3), 270-304.

[325] ZHANG T J. The Correlation between Employer Reciprocity, Employee

Dedication and Corporate Performance - A Statistical Test Based on Private Companies in Jiangsu and Zhejiang. Journal of Guizhou College of Finance and Economics, 2009, (6), 65-69.

[326] Zhang X Y. Research on the Relationship between Perceived Organizational Support, Employee Engagement and Job Performance (Unpublished master's thesis). Wuhan University of Science and Technology, 2013.

[327] ZHANG Y M & GAN Y Q. Chinese version of Utrecht work input scale (UWES) reliability and validity test. Chinese Journal of Clinical Psychology, 2005, 13(3), 268-270.

[328] ZHANG Y, WANG H & FAN J L. Effect of organizational support on resource management practices and employee's performance. Journal of Management Sciences in China, 2008, 11(2), 120-131.

[329] ZHANG Z Y. Scientific Development of Newly Built Universities. Theory and Practice of Education, 2010, 30(1), 58-60.

[330] ZHANG X. China's Education Development and Policy, 1978-2008. Brill, 2011.

[331] ZHAO X Q. Research on the Relationship between Job Stress and Job Performance of Knowledge Workers - Self-efficacy and Coping Strategies as Regulating Variables (Unpublished doctoral thesis). Capital University of Economics and Business, 2012.

[332] ZHENG J J. A Comprehensive Review of Questionnaire Survey. Theory Observe, 2014, (10), 102-103.

[333] ZHENG Y. Job satisfaction, subjective well - being and job performance. Research on Financial and Economic Issues, 2012, (12), 23-30.

[334] ZHOU J M & BAO G M. Social Exchanges in Organizations: From Direct to Indirect Exchanges. Acta Psychologica Sinica, 2005, 37(4), 535-541.

[335] ZHOU M J. Organization, Executive Support, Employee Emotional Commitment and Work Output - A Comparative Study Based on the View of "Exchange of Interests" and "View of Interest Community" (Unpublished doctoral thesis). Zhejiang University, 2005.

[336] ZHOU W J. The problems and Strategies of the newly-built regular colleges' development during the mass higher education process (Unpublished master's thesis). Hunan Normal University, 2009.

[337] ZHUANG X H. Research on the construction of administrative staff in newly - built universities. Theory Research, 2016, 58(1), 80-81.

[338] ZHU H Z & LOU S. Development and reform of higher education in China. Elsevier, 2011.

[339] ZIKMUND W G. Business research methods (7th ed.). Thompson South-Western : Ohio, 2003.

[340] ZIKMUND W G, BABIN B J, CARR J & GRIFFIN M. *Business research methods* (8th ed.). Mason, HO: Cengage Learning, 2010.

APPENDIX 1: Survey Questionnaire

Dear Sir/Madam,

I am a Ph.D. student at Universiti Utara Malaysia, and I am an administrative staff in Yibin University as well. I am conducting a research study on the "Relationship between perceived organizational support, work engagement and job performance of grassroots administrative staff in newly-established universities in Sichuan, China" under the supervision of Dr. Khaliza Binti Saidin. We seek your cooperation in completing the following questionnaire. The questionnaire should take approximately 8-12 minutes to complete. All gathered data are treated with the strictest of confidentiality. Since your personal information does not contain your name, your responses remain absolutely anonymous.

Thank you for your cooperation, and we wish you success in your work.

Best regards.

Peng Wan

Phone: 13350605510

Email: 16798753@qq.com

SECTION A: Demographic Profile of the Respondents

Kindly, tick "√" where necessary and fill in the gap where applicable.

1. Gender:

( ) Male   ( ) Female

2. Age:

( ) Under 30 years   ( ) 30-39 years

( ) 40-49 years   ( ) Above 50 years

3. Marital status:

( ) Unmarried   ( ) Married

4. Education degree:

( ) Diploma   ( ) Bachelor

( ) Master   ( ) Doctoral

5. Academic rank:

( ) Professor or equivalent   ( ) Associate professor or equivalent

( ) Lecturer or equivalent   ( ) Assistant or none

SECTION B: Questionnaire

Please tick "√" in the appropriate box to indicate your level of agreement or disagreement with the following statements according to the scale below.

Strongly Disagree	Disagree	Neutral	Agree	Strongly Agree
1	2	3	4	5

Part 1: Perceived Organizational Support Scale

Items	1	2	3	4	5
1. I can be noticed by the superiors when I am working exceptionally.					
2. The organization attaches special importance to my job objectives and the concept of values.					
3. The organization does not take advantage of me during work as long as there are opportunities.					
4. I can get help from the superiors and colleagues when I have problems at work.					
5. The organization can agree with my reasonable request to change the working conditions or environments.					
6. The organization is happy to help me explore my potential at work.					

Continued

Items	1	2	3	4	5
7. The organization can understand and forgive me for the occasional absence of work for personal reasons.					
8. The organization can reward me for the extra work I have gone beyond the proper duties.					
9. The organization believes it's a large loss to dismiss me.					
10. The organization believes that I will play a great role if it keeps me within the organization.					
11. The organization will employ me if I apply for the job after I has quit.					
12. The organization will never dismiss the employees arbitrarily.					
13. The organization really cares about my living conditions.					
14. The organization can consider the salary I deserve.					
15. The organization can happily provide help when I am in need of special help.					
16. The organization can take the well-being of the employees into consideration at the time of making decision.					
17. The organization will persuade the employees who want to quit to stay.					
18. The organization will transfer me to other positions but not dismiss me if my job cancels.					

SECTION B: Questionnaire

Continued

Items	1	2	3	4	5
19. The organization is proud of the achievements I have made at work.					
20. The organization can pay attention to my opinion at work.					
21. The organization can provide me some opportunities for promotion.					
22. The organization puts me at the positions that I am most suitable for.					
23. The organization can consider increasing our salaries when it obtains more profits.					
24. The organization tries the best to make our work interesting.					

Part 2: Work Engagement Scale

Items	1	2	3	4	5
1. At my work, I feel bursting with energy.					
2. At my job, I feel strong and vigorous.					
3. When I get up in the morning, I feel like going to work.					
4. I am enthusiastic about my job.					
5. My job inspires me.					
6. I am proud of the work that I do.					
7. I feel happy when I am working intensely.					
8. I am immersed in my work.					
9. I get carried away when I'm working.					

Part 3: Job Performance Scale

Items	1	2	3	4	5
1. I finish the work according to the standard operating procedures.					
2. I am familiar with standard operating procedures.					
3. I plan and arrange the schedule of the work I am responsible for.					
4. I pay attention to safety and health problems at work.					
5. I keep the working field tidy and clean.					
6. I put the tools or documents at hand in order and take things back where they were.					
7. My average work efficiency is high.					
8. I am capable of completing all the tasks required by the organization.					
9. I cooperate with others well in the team.					
10. I persist in overcoming obstacles to complete a task.					
11. I volunteer for additional responsibilities.					
12. I follow standard operating procedures and avoid unauthorized shortcuts.					
13. I look for challenging assignments.					
14. I offer to help others accomplish their work.					
15. I pay close attention to important details.					
16. I defend the supervisor's decisions.					
17. I render proper business courtesy.					
18. I support and encourage co-workers with a problem.					
19. I take the initiative to solve a work task.					
20. I exercise personal discipline and self-control.					

SECTION B: Questionnaire

Continued

Items	1	2	3	4	5
21. I tackle a difficult work assignment enthusiastically.					
22. I voluntarily do more than the job requires to help others or contribute to organizational effectiveness.					
23. Overall, I would like to consider the organization and take the initiative to help my coworkers.					